From BASIC to C

Harley M. Templeton

COMPUTE! Publications,Inc.**abc**
One of the ABC Publishing Companies
Greensboro, North Carolina

Copyright 1986, COMPUTE! Publications, Inc. All rights reserved.

Reproduction or translation of any part of this work beyond that permitted by Sections 107 and 108 of the United States Copyright Act without the permission of the copyright owner is unlawful.

Printed in the United States of America

10 9 8 7 6 5 4 3 2

ISBN 0-87455-026-2

The author and publisher have made every effort in the preparation of this book to insure the accuracy of the programs and information. However, the information and programs in this book are sold without warranty, either express or implied. Neither the author nor COMPUTE! Publications, Inc., will be liable for any damages caused or alleged to be caused directly, indirectly, incidentally, or consequentially by the programs or information in this book.

The opinions expressed in this book are solely those of the author and are not necessarily those of COMPUTE! Publications, Inc.

COMPUTE! Publications, Inc., Post Office Box 5406, Greensboro, NC 27403, (919) 275-9809, is one of the ABC Publishing Companies and is not associated with any manufacturer of personal computers. IBM PC and AT are registered trademarks of International Business Machines, Inc. MS-BASIC and MS-DOS are registered trademarks of Microsoft Corporation. Lattice C is a registered trademark of Lattice, Inc. Business-Pro is a registered trademark of Texas Instruments, Inc.

Contents

Foreword vii

Preface ix

Chapter 1. Is There Life After BASIC? 1

Chapter 2. C Language Concepts 7
  Disciplined Programming 9
  C Language Structure 10
  C Language Similarities 12
  Constants 13
  IF-THEN-ELSE Statement 13
  FOR Statement 14
  WHILE Statement 14
  LET Statement 15
  Relational Operators 15
  GOTO Statement 16
  C Language Differences 16
  Top-Down Programming 18
  Conditional Expression 19
  for Statement 19
  else if Statement 20
  switch Statement 20
  do while Statement 21
  continue Statement 21
  C Language Operators 22
  Increment and Decrement Operators 23
  Assignment Operators 23
  Scope of a Variable 23
  Structures 25
  Field Structures 25
  unions 26
  Arrays 27
  Pointers 27
  Input/Output Functions 28

Chapter 3. BASIC Equivalents 31
  Assignment Statement 33
  if Statement 35
  for Loop 37

while Loop	38
goto Statement	39
An Example	40

Chapter 4. Functions 43
- Typical Functions 45
- Functions That Do Not Return a Value 48
- Functions Without Arguments 49
- main Function 50
- Passing Data to a Program 53
- Library Functions 57

Chapter 5. Declarators 59
- Integers 61
- Floating-Point Numbers 62
- Characters and Strings 63
- Special Data Structures 63
- Storage Classes 68

Chapter 6. Arrays and Pointers 75
- Arrays 77
- Strings 78
- Structure Arrays 79
- Pointers 80
- An Array of Pointers 86

Chapter 7. Expressions 91
- Operators 93
- Operator Priority 101
- Expressions 103
- An Example 105

Chapter 8. Transferring Control 107
- else if Statement 109
- for Loop 110
- do while Loop 112
- switch Statement 113
- break Statement 116
- continue Statement 117
- An Example 118

Chapter 9. Input/Output 121
- Displaying Data 124
- More Display Functions 127
- Getting Data from the Keyboard 127
- More Input Functions 129

Sequential File Operations 130
Random File Operations 133
Printing 138
An Illustration 139

Chapter 10. Compiler Control Lines 143
include 146
define 147
undef 151
Conditional Compiling 152
if and endif 152
else 153
ifdef and ifndef 153
An Illustration 154

Chapter 11. Finishing Touches 159
Completing Your Program 161
Compiling Your Program 161
Linking Your Program 162
Running Your Program 164
Compiler Details 164
LINK Utility Details 165
Response File 166
Library Files 167
Link Map 168
Error Messages 170
Debugging Your Program 174
Using DEBUG 182

Appendices 187
A. C Language Summary 189
B. Hexadecimal Numbers 193
C. ASCII Code 199
D. Microprocessor Addressing 201

Index 205

Foreword

Now that you feel confident programming in BASIC and have done as much as you can within BASIC's limits, it's time to move on. Maybe you have even done advanced programming in machine language on your personal computer. C is the next step.

Why C? And why this book?

The personal computer field is a fast-paced, ever-changing environment. Once you've mastered and written programs for one computer, a new, more-powerful system comes along. One approach many programmers have taken is to translate their most important programs from BASIC or machine language on one machine to the newer model. Although this may be a learning experience, it can quickly become tiresome.

C is perhaps the most transportable language yet for personal computer programmers. Often a C program written for one computer can be transported to another computer by simply copying the source code to the new computer and recompiling.

For anyone who knows BASIC, *From BASIC to C* is the logical way to learn C easily and quickly. By using the knowledge you already have, *From BASIC to C* teaches you how to program in C. It doesn't waste time teaching concepts and techniques you already have, but *uses* your knowledge of BASIC and *builds* on it. Using numerous program examples, *From BASIC to C* shows you how to get the results you want.

The first chapters discuss in clear, easy-to-understand terms the concepts needed to program in C, and pay special attention to those ideas which differ from BASIC. Later sections present C equivalents to BASIC statements and routines.

From BASIC to C includes everything you need to know to begin writing C programs, from compiler control instructions to macros to I/O routines. We've even included scores of program examples and routines you can adapt and add to your own programs.

As with all COMPUTE! publications, *From BASIC to C* is written in the easy-to-understand style you've come to expect. This may be the only C guide you'll ever need.

Preface

This book is for the personal computer owner who has learned to program in BASIC, and who wants to learn to program in C. It is for anyone who has attained a good working knowledge of BASIC. If you want to learn this language, either to be able to program as a hobbyist or as a professional, this book is for you. The efficiency of the C programming language and the portability of programs written in C lend themselves to software development; the age of the software entrepreneur is not past.

Because C requires a more rigorous approach than BASIC, I've devoted an entire chapter of this book to presenting the concepts of the C programming language. One chapter discusses C statements that are very similar to BASIC statements, showing an example of a program that consists entirely of these statements. Subsequent chapters discuss the additional capabilities of C. The last chapter discusses compiling, linking, and debugging C programs, with detailed information on debugging, a major problem for someone learning C.

The chapters are arranged in a logical sequence, but perhaps not the best sequence in which to read them. If you have a compiler and can compile the examples as you read, you should read Chapter 11 right after Chapter 1. Chapter 11 tells how to compile your program so that you can try the examples as you go. Because I/O is an important part of any practical program, you may want to read Chapter 9 next so that you can add more sophisticated I/O to some of the examples.

Since C is a highly transportable language, most of the book applies to all implementations. Certain sections are written for the user of the IBM PC, AT, and the many compatible and nearly compatible personal computers. Appendix D includes addressing information for both the microprocessor in the PC and the one in the AT. The system dependencies assumed in the book are those of MS-DOS. The specific compiler described is the Lattice C Compiler.

During the writing of the book, a C Program Language interpreter and a number of new C compilers have come on the market. Several are significantly less expensive than the Lattice C Compiler. The language portion of this book applies to the interpreters and compilers to the extent that they conform to the C language definition in *The C Programming Language*, by Brian W. Kernighan and Dennis M. Ritchie, which has become a de facto standard. Information about compiling does not apply to the interpreters and differs among compilers. Debugging an interpreted program is entirely different from debugging a compiled program. The standard library functions should be similar to those described here, although the function library supplied with less expensive compilers may not be as comprehensive as that supplied with Lattice C.

I am grateful to those who helped in the production of the book. In particular, I am deeply grateful for the understanding and patience of my sweet wife Shirley. Her tolerance of my becoming absorbed in my writing has made this book possible.

It is my hope that this book will assist you in achieving your goal of becoming an effective C language programmer.

Chapter 1

Is There Life After BASIC?

Chapter 1
Is There Life After BASIC?

So you can make your computer do anything you want it to in BASIC? You've got a good background in the BASIC language. Congratulations! What's next?

Why not learn a professional programming language? Some programmers say, "Real programmers don't write in BASIC. Actually, no programmers write in BASIC after the age of 12." While that is just a weak attempt at humor, BASIC does have limitations, and learning the C language will introduce you to a different brand of programming. Maybe it is time now to leave the joys of a carefree BASIC behind? Writing your BASIC programs has taught you a lot about programming. Much of what you learned programming in BASIC applies to any programming language. You can build on what you have learned and prepare yourself for more effective programming.

Have you ever noticed that BASIC is slow? That is because BASIC is not usually compiled; it is interpreted. When BASIC is interpreted, each statement is translated into the ones and zeros that the microprocessor in your computer understands. This process is repeated each time the statement is executed. A FOR-NEXT loop may cause a set of statements to be repeated many times. The interpreter doesn't remember what it has done; the translation process is performed for each statement each time through the loop. Sometimes the translation takes longer than the operation requested in the statement. Translation always takes a significant portion of the total time to run a program.

The C language, on the other hand, is usually compiled. When a language is compiled, its statements are not directly executed by the computer. Instead, you write them to a file, called the *source program*. The source program is processed by the compiler, a program or pair of programs that translate the

Chapter 1

statements of the source program into an *object program*. The object program consists of the *machine instructions* (the good old ones and zeros) that the microprocessor understands. The object program is processed by the link program to produce the *executable program* (Figure 1-1).

The computer can execute the finished program much more quickly than the BASIC interpreter can translate and execute its program. The time required to run the object program is the actual time it takes the computer to perform the machine instructions. This makes it possible for you to do things in C for which BASIC is too slow.

Take a closer look at Figure 1-1. Notice that the compiler looks for errors in the source program. When it finds errors, correct the errors and compile again. When the compiler finds no more errors, you are ready for the next step, linking. Your program may call existing programs, either some you have previously compiled or some of the standard programs. The link program obtains the object programs your program needs from one or more libraries and combines them into the executable program.

Your program may not be free of errors at this point; the compiler has no way of knowing what you want your program to do. You must try to run the executable program, testing it for errors. If you find any, you must again correct the source program, recompile, relink, and try the program again. This may seem like a lot of unnecessary compiling and linking. The final result, however, is well worth the effort.

This book presents the statements of the C programming language as they relate to BASIC. It is not a comprehensive description of the language. You will also need a reference book. *The C Programming Language* by Brian W. Kernighan and Dennis M. Ritchie (Prentice-Hall, Englewood Cliffs, NJ, 1978) has become the de facto standard for the language, probably because one of its authors wrote C. However, this book is not for the beginner; it assumes that you already are a programmer. You will also need the manual that comes with your compiler to give you details that apply to your particular computer.

Kernighan and Ritchie are correct when they say that you must learn a programming language by programming in it. This book contains many C programming examples. You should have access to a computer with a C compiler so that

Figure 1-1. Developing a C Language Program

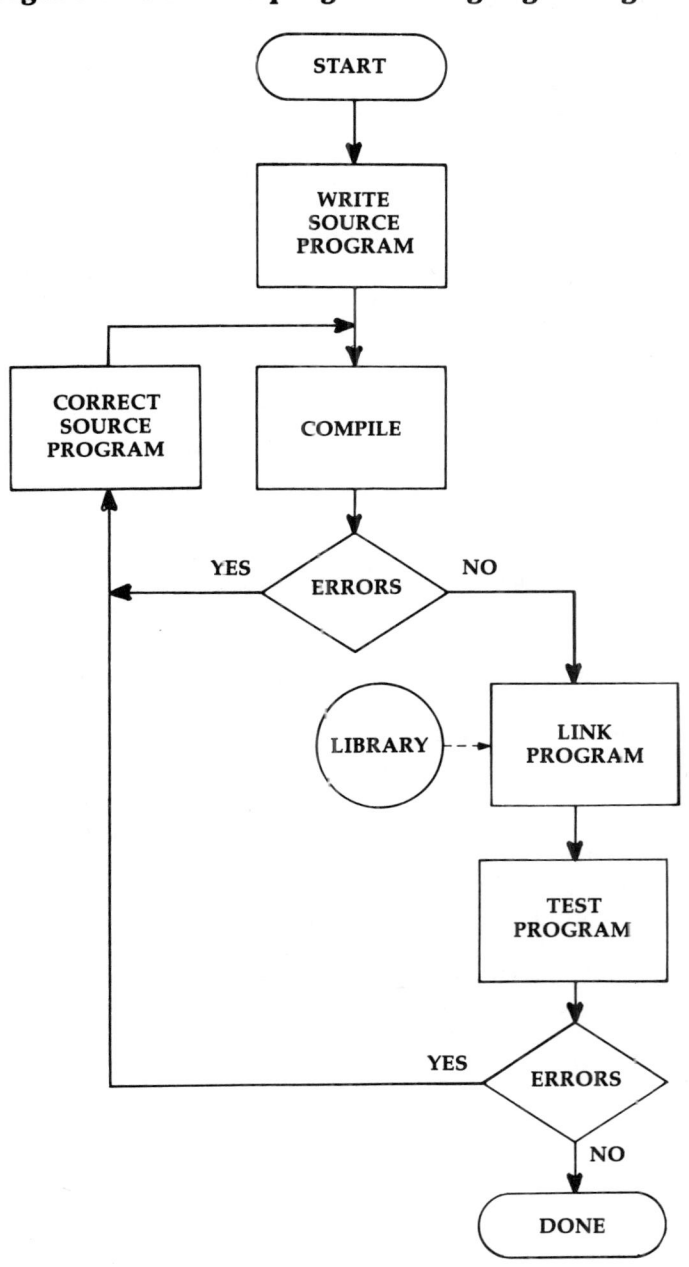

Chapter 1

you can compile and run these examples as well as programs of your own.

A word about the program examples. The program examples listed in this book fall into four groups. The first group includes program fragments which are intended as illustrations and will not compile. The second group contains program fragments that will compile, but will not link or execute properly. The third group includes program segments that, when correctly combined with other segments, will compile, link, and run. The final group gives complete program source code that will compile, link, and run. As you read through the text, those examples that will compile, link, and run are identified. If the text does not specifically state that an example will compile, link, and execute, you should assume that it is an illustration and will not compile.

This book begins by describing the concepts of the C language. It then presents an overview of the similarities and differences between BASIC and C. Next is a detailed description of similarities, with examples of each similar statement. Finally, it describes the differences in detail, also with examples. The last chapter in the book tells you how to compile, link, and debug your programs. If you have a C compiler at your disposal, you should skip to the last chapter and learn how to compile and link your programs at this point. Then as you return to Chapter 2, you can try out the examples as you go.

Yes, there is life after BASIC. Another author has said that C is too complex for anyone to learn from a book. Don't be discouraged. The big advantage of learning in a class is the discipline provided by the classroom situation. You actually do the learning, whether in a class or from a book. You can learn C if you study it and apply what you learn by compiling and running the examples. Then when you write, compile, and use your own programs, you gain experience and more knowledge of the language. It's up to you.

Chapter 2

C Language Concepts

Chapter 2
C Language Concepts

The concepts of C are quite different from those of BASIC. Some of the difference is related to the histories of the languages. Although it is not highly thought of in academic circles today, BASIC was written by college professors as a beginning language for their programming students. C was written by a researcher at Bell Laboratories, primarily for his own use and for use in the laboratories. Because there was no pressure to get it on the market, he was able to fine-tune it and produce a language that did exactly the type of job the author wanted.

When C eventually became available outside Bell Labs, its advantages made it popular. First, it's a professional programming language, small enough to be readily learned, but structured and disciplined enough to be efficient. Second, it is nearly as flexible as machine language, allowing you to write almost any program as directly as you can in machine language. But perhaps the most important advantage C has is *transportability*. This means that few, if any, changes to your program have to be made when you use the program on a computer other than the one for which it was written. These advantages all add up to make C the language of choice for many programmers.

One problem that limits the transportability of C programs is that no standard for the language has been adopted. A committee of the American National Standards Institute (ANSI) is currently working out the final details of a proposed standard. Since lack of a standard definition for the language has produced a standard by default, the ANSI standard will probably be ignored, as was the ANSI standard for BASIC.

Disciplined Programming

BASIC is a means of getting your computer to do something; it helps you by being informal and requiring a minimum of structure and restrictions. C, like other professional programming

Chapter 2

languages, has structure and restrictions that develop a disciplined approach to writing programs. This is not to make things difficult for you, nor is it to separate the hobbyists from the professionals. It's necessary to efficiently produce and maintain the software we need if our computers are to do useful things.

Twenty years ago many programs were written to impress people with their complexity. The idea was that if you showed the boss a complex program, he or she would assume that anyone who could figure that out and make it work was only slightly short of being a genius. However, if the writer of a program left the company, another programmer often had to start over when the program needed to be changed. It promoted job security for the programmer, but was not good for the industry in the long run.

Today, an increasing number of people know that a readable program is more useful than a cryptic one. Supervisors recognize instructions put in just to make the program look complicated. And they want a program that any qualified programmer can pick up and finish if the current programmer decides to go somewhere else. A structured programming language results in better understanding of the program. When the program lists all variables that it uses at the head of each structure, it's a lot easier for anyone to figure out what it does. So the discipline built into C pays off when you program for a living.

C Language Structure

It's probably not intuitively obvious to you what I mean by *structure*, because BASIC has very little structure. You always have a line number, the statement extends to the first colon or to the end of the line, and that's about it. A BASIC subroutine, beginning at the line specified in the GOSUB statement and ending at a RETURN statement, is about as close as BASIC comes to the C *function*, which typifies C programming structure.

A C language function includes the names for data items used in the function as well as the statements that perform the operations required. The function is the building block of a C program.

Here's what a function looks like:

C Language Concepts

```
chwr(c) /* Write character */
char c;
{
int ch;
if ((ch = putc(c,fpo)) == EOF) {
  printf("Write error writing character %c.\n",c);
  exit( );
  }
}
```

(As stated in Chapter 1, most program examples in this book will not compile without more code being added, but are included as illustrations only. Program code that will compile and link is so stated.)

Within a function you can use another structure: a *compound statement*, or *block*, as in the **if** statement of the function example. A compound statement is a group of statements enclosed in braces and used as if it were a single statement. In BASIC's IF-THEN-ELSE statement, you can have statements within the IF-THEN statement and more statements in the ELSE portion. The statements are separated by colons and must all fit within the maximum size allowed for a line. In C, you can use a block of statements for either the THEN or the ELSE portion (or both).

As an example, you might have this line in a BASIC program:

50 IF A < C THEN A = C: B = C ELSE A = 5: B = 5

The C equivalent includes two blocks, like this:

```
if (a < c) {
  a = c;
  b = c;
  }
else {
  a = 5;
  b = 5;
  }
```

Each block is enclosed in braces, and may contain as many statements as you wish. A block may also contain data items that appear in the block. The function and the block are examples of the structure of C.

Another efficiency that results from the discipline of the C language is that functions can be stored in libraries and used

Chapter 2

in many different programs. A *library* is a special type of file that contains object files of compiled functions. Writing another program may consist primarily of selecting existing functions from those you have already written, writing a few new ones, and combining them in the new program. As discussed in Chapter 1, the link program makes one executable program from an object program and the functions it calls. Except for new functions, the program has already been compiled and tested.

Listing all the variables may seem like a drag. In BASIC, you just use the variable in an assignment statement, and it is defined. You don't even have to use a DIM statement for an array unless the value of a dimension exceeds 10. But if you ever need to know whether a particular variable name is already in use, you have a job on your hands. The longer the program, the bigger the job. Not only that, but if you ever want to combine parts of various programs, you must know the names and types of variables in each part. So, in the long run, having to list all the variables really helps you.

When you consider going from BASIC to a professional programming language that enforces discipline in your programs, you have a choice to make. Doing it the BASIC way may be the easy way, but doing it the disciplined way results in programming efficiency. This may not be important when you write programs as a hobby, but it pays off when you write programs for a living. And it is essential when you are employed as a programmer.

C Language Similarities

Even though you must list them in advance, you'll feel right at home with C *variable names*. As in BASIC, a variable name must start with a letter, but it may contain either letters or numbers after the first character. The letters must be lowercase, though. See, you know something about C language already.

However, the *types* of variables are more important than they are in BASIC. A string variable has to be specified in BASIC, by using a dollar sign ($) at the end of the variable name. Otherwise, you usually don't have to worry about the type of a variable. In C, you use a statement called a *declarator* when you list a variable. The declarator identifies the variable as an integer (**int**), a real number (**float**), or a string (**char**).

C Language Concepts

Here are some declarators:

`int hours, rate;`

`float earnings;`

`char ml[ ] = "Your total pay is ";`

It's really easier to use declarators, because you don't have to figure out the variable's type when something doesn't come out quite as you wanted. And because you declared a variable properly, you are more likely to use it correctly.

Constants

Constants, too, are the same in both BASIC and C. But C has an additional type of constant: the *character constant*, which is just a one-character string (Lattice C allows as many as four characters in a character constant). You can declare a character constant like this:

`char s = 's';`

Like BASIC, C stores a string constant in memory in a way that tells the computer how many characters are in the string. Specifically, the C compiler stores a *null character* (zero) at the end of each string. Here's the declarator of a single-character string:

`char ess[ ] = "s";`

This stores two characters in memory: an *s* and a null (\0, having a value of zero).

Both string *ess* and character "s" contain the character *s*. The string also contains the null character to indicate the end of the string. A character constant and a string constant consisting of the same character are not interchangeable.

IF-THEN-ELSE Statement

The BASIC IF-THEN-ELSE statement provides a two-way branch in your program. C's **if else** statement is very similar, as was previously shown in the example of the compound statement. As in BASIC, the **if** is followed by an expression, often a relational expression. The value of the expression, true or false, determines which part of the statement is executed. As in BASIC, the **else** portion is optional. When it is omitted and the value of the expression is false, the **if** statement is not executed, and control passes to the next statement.

Chapter 2

FOR Statement

C also has a **for** statement, but it's more explicit than BASIC's FOR statement. The STEP is never implied; it's stated, but not as a step. No NEXT statement is required; either a statement or a compound statement is performed for each value of the counting variable. The structure of the statement or compound statement defines the limit without a NEXT.

The MS-BASIC FOR loop looks like this:

```
60 FOR I = 1 TO 10 STEP 2
70 A = I * A
80 PRINT A
90 NEXT I
```

You would write the loop like this in C:

```
for (i = 1;i <= 10; i = i + 2) {
   a = i * a;
   printf ("%d\n",a);
}
```

The loops both work alike. The initial value is compared to the final value before the statements in the loop are performed. The statements in the loop are performed only if the values make it appropriate to do so. (Some versions of BASIC perform the statements in the loop at least once.)

WHILE Statement

The **while** statement of C is exactly like the WHILE statement of BASIC. It's followed by either a statement or a compound statement, and doesn't require a WEND statement to close the loop. In BASIC, the WHILE statement looks like this:

```
70 WHILE X < 6
80    X = X + 1
90    PRINT X
100 WEND
```

The C version is this:

```
while (x < 6)
   printf("%d\n",++x);
```

The two versions work exactly alike, but the C example very nicely combines the two statements into one. In both cases, the loops print the value of X + 1, incrementing X by 1 until X + 1 is equal to 6. If the initial value of X is greater than 5, neither program prints X + 1.

C Language Concepts

LET Statement
The simple assignment statement is also like the assignment statement of BASIC. LET is not optional; it's not even allowed. Your BASIC program might contain these statements:

10 LET X = 0
20 Y = X

You could do the same thing in C:

x = 0;
y = 0;

Or you could do it all with this statement:

x = y = 0;

The rightmost item does not have to be a constant; it can be an expression. However, the left-to-right order is important. The C program first sets y to zero, then x to y. The expression on the right determines the value assigned to each of the variables to the left.

Arithmetic expressions are very similar, too, but the MOD operator of BASIC is replaced by the percent sign (%). The operator for division is the slash (/), even if an integer result is required. If the result is a real number, it must be forced to an integer type when an integer is required.

Instead of these statements:

100 YEARS% = MONTHS% / 12
110 MONTHS% = MONTHS% MOD 12

The C version could be:

int months, years;
years = months / 12;
months = months % 12;

Relational Operators
C relational operators are identical to those of BASIC, except for equal and not equal. BASIC uses the same equal sign as a relational operator and as the assignment operator. C uses the equal sign as an assignment operator only; it uses two equal signs (==) for the equal relational operator. The not equal relational operator of C is exclamation point equal sign (!=).

You could have these IF statements in your BASIC program:

200 IF X = 7 THEN Y = Z
210 IF A <> Y THEN A = Z

15

Chapter 2

The equivalent **if** statements are:

```
if (x == 7) /* x = 7 would set x to 7! Not an error! */
   y = z;
if (a != y)
   a = z;
```

GOTO Statement

BASIC's GOTO statement is not very popular with some professional programmers. The structure of C makes a GOTO statement unnecessary, and seldom wanted. However the C language includes a **goto** statement. Since, C has no line numbers, you'll need a label to tell the program which statement to execute next. The label used in the **goto** statement must appear, followed by a colon, before a statement.

This BASIC statement branches unconditionally to line 900:

800 GOTO 900

The C equivalent is:

```
goto end;
```

The statement to which you intend to branch must have a label:

```
end: return;
```

All these items in the C language are either like those you already know about in BASIC or they are very similar. Learning this new language is not going to be so bad after all. Chapter 3 contains detailed information about these statements, with some more examples.

C Language Differences

There is nothing in BASIC that is quite like the *function* of C. Here's another example:

```
fcomma(buff) /* Locate first comma in buff */
char *buff;
{
int i = 0;
while (buff[i] != ',')
   i++;
return (i);
}
```

C Language Concepts

A function is a structure, beginning with a name and a list of arguments (if any) passed to it by the calling function. The argument in the example is *buff*. Next come the *declarators* for the arguments. The **char** declarator tells the compiler what type of argument to expect. The declarators for the variables, structures, and functions internal to the function come next. In the example, **int** variable *i* is the only one. The declarator initializes the variable; this is optional. The remainder of the function is a group of statements or compound statements (blocks) to be executed. The example has only one: a **while** statement. Like the built-in functions of BASIC, a C function can return a value, which replaces the function call in the statement that calls the function. The example returns *i*, the location of the first comma within string *buff*.

A C program is itself a function. It includes calls to other functions of the program. Every executable statement in the program is either a part of the *main( )* function (the program) or a part of a function called (directly or indirectly) by the *main( )* function. To put it another way, each of the functions that make up the program is called by a statement in the *main( )* function or in another function of the program.

In many instances, you could write the entire program as a single function, but you really do not want to. By properly analyzing the program, you can identify portions that are executed more than once. These portions should be functions for two reasons. First, you have less of a program to write (and to debug) when you call an existing function instead of writing a portion of the program again. Second, you can usually write the function so that you can use it in future programs. In that case, part of the future program is already written and debugged.

Even when you use a portion of the code only once, using a separate function is still a good idea. Having the function available for future use is one good reason; making the program easier to maintain is another. When the *main( )* function (the program) just calls other functions, each of which performs a well-defined portion of the entire task, what the program does becomes obvious. When something goes wrong, you have the appropriate function to debug, not the entire program.

Program maintenance is not so important to a hobbyist. The same person often writes and maintains a program. It is no one else's business what it takes to fix it. Don't fall into

Chapter 2

that trap. Once you have finished a program and started using it, you'll be surprised how quickly you forget what you did. You'll find yourself wishing you had organized the program more logically so that you can readily find the trouble. And take it from one who found out the hard way: A program that has been working well for months *does* sometimes have to be debugged.

Top-Down Programming

Organizing your program into functions is a different approach that you must learn with C. It's not difficult, though, and it is well worth the trouble. The easiest way is to follow the techniques of "top-down programming." First, identify the variables that your program requires, then list them, either as complete C declarators or just as a list. Next, divide the processing your program will perform into large sections and list these major sections. For many programs, your list will be similar to this:

1. Request filenames and select options (menu)
2. Read data
3. Perform required processing
4. Write processed data

Now do the same thing for each of the major sections. Here, the lists become less general and more specific. But the principle is the same. Break each major section into identifiable portions, each of which is more manageable.

For some programs, these portions will be the lowest level in the program structure. In other cases, they should be divided further. Eventually, however, you'll have identified everything that the program must do, providing the complete structure of your program.

Examine the program structure, looking for identical portions, or portions that can be made identical by being a bit more general. When several portions are identical, the function that the identical portions perform can be programmed as a single function.

At this point, your *main( )* function is clearly defined. Assign names to the major sections and write the *main( )* function, calling the functions that correspond to the sections. Then, for each section, identify and list the variables, and name the portions of the program that will become functions

C Language Concepts

to be called. Then write the function for each section. Thus, working from the *top down*, you continue until the entire program is completed.

Right about now you may be feeling that you have done a lot of work before actually starting to program. That depends upon what you mean by programming. Actually, everything you have done is a part of the programming process. You have planned the structure of your program rather than just letting it grow. This provides several benefits. First, you have identified functions that apply in several portions of your program. These functions need to be written only once. Second, you can debug the program functions one at a time. Once each function is doing its job accurately, you know that additional errors are in other parts of the program. And last of all, should you have to change the program, you'll need to change only some of the functions, not the entire program.

Conditional Expression

So much for the general differences between BASIC and C. Are you ready for specifics? The C programming language has a new construction called the *conditional expression* that's very handy. It's like a condensed IF statement for limited uses, but you'll find enough uses for it to make it valuable. It consists of three expressions, only two of which are evaluated in any one execution of the statement. When the first expression (often a relational expression) is true, the conditional expression takes the value of the second expression. When the first expression is false, the value of the third expression applies. In your BASIC program, you might have this statement:

350 IF A > 9 THEN D = A/10 ELSE D = A

Assigning the value of a conditional statement to variable D does the same thing in C. It looks like this:

d = (a>9)? a/10: a;

Pretty slick, eh? The details are in Chapter 7; for now, when (*a>9*) is true, *d* is set to *a/10*. When (*a>9*) is false, *d* is set to *a*.

for Statement

One form of the **for** statement is very similar to BASIC:

for (i = 1;i <= 6;i = i + 1)

Index variable *i* is initialized to 1, and the statement or block that follows is executed for each value of *i* from 1 to 6. Stated formally, this type of loop uses a series of values of *i* that are an *arithmetic progression*. Unlike BASIC, the **for** statement is not limited to loops that use arithmetic progressions. How about a *geometric progression*?

```
for (i = 1; i <= 100000; i = i * 10)
```

Or maybe more than one variable?

```
for (i = 1, j = 6; i <= 6; i = i + 1, j = j - 1)
```

The details are in Chapter 8. Are you beginning to see why you should learn the C language?

else if Statement

The **else if** option of the **if** statement provides a way of branching to one of several statements:

```
if (x == 1)
    y = 7;
  else if (x == 2)
    y = 5;
      else if (x == 3)
        y = 4;
          else
            y = 1;
```

This is really not so different from BASIC. You could do the same thing in BASIC provided that all of your IF statement would fit on one program line. But here you see the advantage of the structure C requires: From this structure it's much easier to see what is being done than it would be from the equivalent BASIC statement. The details of **else if** are in Chapter 8.

switch Statement

C has another way to branch to one of several statements, the **switch** statement:

```
switch (x) {
  case 1:
    y = 7;
    break;
  case 2:
    y = 5;
    break;
```

C Language Concepts

```
    case 3:
        y = 4;
        break;
    default:
        y = 1;
        break;
}
```

This example does exactly the same thing as the **else if** example. The **switch** statement is discussed in detail in Chapter 8. At this point, notice the prefixes **case** and **default** that go with the statement. Notice also the **break** statement. It transfers control from the block that follows **switch**, also preventing execution of the remaining statements.

do while Statement

MS-BASIC does not provide a loop that is always executed once, a loop in which the test is performed after the first time through the statements in the loop instead of before. That is what the **do while** loop of C is for:

```
do {
    a=a+1;
    b=b-1;
}
while (b>0);
```

In this example, *a* is incremented and *b* is decremented even if *b* is zero or less to start with. Further information on the **do while** statement is in Chapter 8.

continue Statement

You can use the **continue** statement within any C program loop (**for**, **while**, or **do**) to skip the remaining statements in the loop and begin the loop again. You would use the GOTO statement of BASIC, and the line number would be that of the WEND or NEXT statement. Here's an example in BASIC:

```
300 X = 0
310 WHILE X <= 6
320    X = X + 1
330    IF Y(X) < 5 THEN GOTO 350
340    YTOT = YTOT + Y(X)
350 WEND
```

Chapter 2

Examine this:

```
x=0;
while (x<=6) {
  x=x+1;
  if (y[x]<5)
    continue;
  ytot=ytot+y[x];
}
```

As you have probably figured out by now, y[x] is an element of array y. The loop totals y[1] through y[6], ignoring values less than 5. The **continue** statement skips over the assignment statement that accumulates the total when an element of the array is less than 5. Details of the **continue** statement are in Chapter 8.

C Language Operators

Altogether, C uses more operators than BASIC, but it has fewer logical operators. The **&&** operator corresponds to the AND operator, the II operator corresponds to OR, and the ! operator corresponds to NOT. But there is a difference. In MS-BASIC, the logical operators perform a bit-by-bit logical operation on corresponding bits of integers. This provides a valid logical result when you use −1 for true, but produces an incorrect result with some values. In C, the operands are considered to be true if their values are not equal to 0. The value of a relational expression is either 0 (false) or +1 (true). You can perform the missing operations (EQV, IMP, and XOR for expressions) with proper combinations of **&&**, II, and !. You probably never use them, anyway.

C has bit-by-bit operations, too. The bit-by-bit operators are **&** (AND), I (OR), ^ (XOR), and ~ (NOT); these apply to the bits of integers.

The C language also provides shift operators, which shift the bits of integers. The left shift operator is << and the right shift operator is >>. The integer expression precedes the operator, and the number of bit positions shifted follows the operator. Shift operations are used to format bits for bit operations, and for quick multiplication and division of integers when the multiplier or divisor is a power of two. For example, a right shift of one bit divides the integer by two. A left shift of two bits multiplies by four.

C Language Concepts

Increment and Decrement Operators
Two powerful features of C are the increment (++) and decrement (--) operators. In some of the previous examples, I wrote i++ instead of i = i + 1, and j-- instead of j = j - 1. You can put the operator in front of the variable name as a *prefix* or following it as a *postfix*. When you use ++ as a prefix, incrementing is performed before the variable is used in another operation. When you use it as a postfix, the variable is incremented after the other operation. Similarly, -- as a prefix specifies decrementing first, and -- as a postfix means decrementing after the other operation.

Assignment Operators
Another shortcut available in C is a set of additional assignment operators. Besides =, the language uses +=, -=, *=, /=, %=, <<=, >>=, &=, |=, and ^=. For example, the following statements give the same result:

a = a + b;

a += b;

Similarly, the combination of other operators with = means to perform the operation on the two operands and set the left operand to the value of the result.

All of the operators described briefly here are fully described in Chapter 7.

Scope of a Variable
Every variable in a C program has an attribute called *scope*. The only instance of this concept in BASIC is in a user-defined function. Do you recall that the dummy arguments in a DEF FN statement apply only within that statement? Another way to say this is to say that the scope of the dummy arguments is the function definition. All other variables in a BASIC program have a scope that extends to the entire program. In C, the scope of a variable declared in a block is the block within which it is declared. When a variable is declared within a function (but not within a block in the function), the scope is the entire function. A variable declared outside any function has a scope that includes the entire source file; that scope can be extended to include the entire program.

Figure 2-1 illustrates the scopes of the variables in a program. Notice that the variables declared before the *main()*

function (*fp*, *fnam*, and *n*) are valid in the entire program (assuming that the entire source program is in one file). Thus, any reference to *n* anywhere in the program refers to the integer defined on the fourth line of the program. (However, if another variable *n* was declared within a function of the program, any reference to *n* in that function would access the new variable.)

Figure 2-1. Scope of Variables

```
#include <stdio.h>
FILE *fopen( ), *fp;   /* The scope of these variables */
char fnam[6];          /* includes the entire program */
int n = 0;
.
.
.
main( )         /* Main function begins here */
{
int x, y, z;    /* The scope of these variables is the */
char ch;        /* Main function only */
while (n < 50) { /* Start of block */
int x, y;       /* The scope of these variables is */
.               /* this block only */
.
.
}               /* End of block */
.
.
.
return;         /* End of main function */
}
```

Another set of variables is defined in the *main( )* function. These variables, except *x* and *y*, apply in the entire *main( )* function. The block of the **while** statement defines integers *x* and *y* also. Within that block, any reference to *x* or *y* refers to the variables defined in the block, not to those defined for the *main( )* function.

The scope concept is not something added just to make C harder to learn. It works closely with the structure of a C language program to help you understand the program better. You do not have contention between variables with the same name in different functions when each has its own function as

C Language Concepts

its scope. Often, having to use a different name for a different variable that is functionally the same complicates the program. When each variable has its boundaries (scope), related variables can have the same name.

Structures

Have you ever wanted a way to define a set of related data items of different lengths and types? For example, you might have a mailing list with a name, street and number, city and state, zip code, expiration date, and selection code for each address on the list. If the items are all strings, you can do it in BASIC with a six-element string array. But if the selection code and expiration date are used as integers (for selection and for computing other dates, perhaps), you have to convert string to integer, and back again. And you have to remember which element of the array is the item you want.

C has a solution to the problem. Declare a *structure* for the mailing list:

```
struct {
  char name[20];
  char street[15];
  char city[20];
  char zip[5];
  int date;
  int code;
} member;
```

This declaration identifies *member* as a structure. The variables in the structure are *member.name, member.street, member.city, member.zip, member.date,* and *member.code.* The first four variables are strings, and the numbers in brackets are the maximum numbers of characters in the strings.

The structure helps you keep track of the variables in the structure, but you must access each variable individually. C does not have a statement that moves an entire structure from one location in memory to another.

Field Structures

The *code* variable can be very useful. Suppose the member mailing list includes life members, new members, paid-up members, and associate members. If you could assign a different bit in the variable for each of these categories, you could

Chapter 2

use the code to select names of members in one or more categories for a special mailing. C provides a way to declare a structure for an integer that divides it into *fields*. A field can consist of one or more bits. This is one way you could declare variable *code:*

```
struct {
  unsigned life : 1;
  unsigned new : 1;
  unsigned paid_up : 1;
  unsigned associate : 1;
} code;
```

You should define this structure within the *address* structure; use this declaration instead of

```
int code;
```

This structure provides a way to set, reset, or test each of these bits. The combined structures *(address* and *code)* give you names for each bit: *member.code.life, member.code.new, member.code.paid_up,* and *member.code.associate.*

unions

The **union** is another new data structure. It's used to hold variables of different types. At different times during program execution, a program might need to have a single location that may contain an integer, a long integer, or a double-precision floating-point value. You can declare a **union** for that purpose:

```
union {
  int count;
  long int total;
  float percent;
} number;
```

The example declares a memory location labeled *number* that can contain either a *count,* a *total,* or a *percent.* It may be convenient for these values to share one location, assuming that only one of the three is required at any one time. However, the *count* is an integer value, the *total* (being too large to fit in an integer) is a long integer, and the *percent* is type **float**, a real number (decimal fraction). The compiler assigns different numbers of bytes to each of these types. The **union** declarator tells the compiler to assign a location for *number* that meets the size requirements for all three variables. Your program must keep track of the type of variable in the location at all times.

26

C Language Concepts

Arrays
At a glance, C arrays are identical to BASIC arrays, but there are subtle differences. The equivalent to a DIM statement in BASIC is a declaration in C:

90 OPTION BASE 1
100 DIM A%(5, 10)

int a[5][10];

The DIM statement and the declaration both define two-dimensional arrays with five rows and ten columns. Because of the OPTION BASE 1 statement, the rows of the BASIC array are numbered 1–5, and the columns are numbered 1–10. The C array rows are 0–4, and columns are 0–9. Otherwise, the arrays are alike.

To assign a value to an element of array *a*, use a statement like this:

a[1][4] = b * 25;

Pointers
The C language has a data item that has no counterpart in BASIC: the *pointer*. A pointer is the address of a data item. Pointers are needed when a function has to alter the value of a variable in another function. Variables passed to a function from the calling function are copies of the variables. Whatever the function does to a variable has no effect on the value of that variable in the calling function. Some functions need to alter values of variables in the calling function; they do it with pointers.

A declaration tells the C compiler that *px* is a pointer. An example declaration is:

int *px;

In this example, *px* is a pointer to an integer. You can interpret the declarator as if it said, "The contents of address *px* is an integer." The compiler must know how many bytes the item at that address occupies. The declaration of the pointer as a pointer to an integer tells the compiler that the item occupies two bytes.

You must place an address in the pointer; a statement like this is one way to do it:

px = &x;

Chapter 2

The statement that places an address in the pointer can be read, "*px* is the address of *x*." It gives the pointer a value.

The C language can access an element of an array with a pointer:

a = *(px + 2);

When *px* is a pointer to array *x*, this example assigns the value of element 2 of the array to variable *a*, using *address arithmetic* (or *pointer arithmetic*). It is different from most arithmetic because it does not necessarily mean "the address of *x* plus two bytes." What it really means is "the address of *x* plus two elements of array *x*." The declaration of *px* states that *px* is a pointer to an integer which occupies two bytes. So the address of the integer that is assigned to *a* is *px* + four bytes. If *px* was a pointer to a real number which occupies four bytes, *px* + 2 would mean *px* + eight bytes.

This chapter just introduces the new concepts of the C language that apply to data items. Chapters 5 and 6 describe these concepts in detail.

Input/Output Functions

One more difference between BASIC and C is input/output. BASIC includes input/output statements like INPUT and PRINT, with variations. C doesn't have input/output statements. Instead, your C compiler package includes one or more standard C libraries. These contain standard input/output functions, functions that interface with MS-DOS (or whatever operating system applies to your compiler). In a C program, you call standard functions to perform input and output.

Some of the examples shown in this chapter show calls to **putc( )** and **printf( )**, two of the standard input/output functions. The following program displays a prompt, reads the response, and displays the response. This example will compile, link, and run. It uses **printf( )** to display the prompt and again to display the result. It uses **gets( )** to read the response. Chapter 9 describes these functions in detail.

C Language Concepts

```
#include <stdio.h>
main( ) /* Respond to prompt */
{
char name[31]; /* 30 characters maximum */

printf("Type in your first name: ");
gets(name);
printf("\n%s",name);
}
```

    This chapter has presented the similarities and differences of C and BASIC as an overview intended to challenge you to learn this more powerful language. Don't be discouraged as you wonder how you'll ever learn all these new ideas. BASIC presented a lot of ideas that were new to you when you learned it. C uses these ideas (although some of them are used differently) and adds new ones. The remaining chapters of this book describe these ideas fully. Learn them one at a time. You'll find that learning C is worth the effort.

Chapter 3
BASIC Equivalents

Chapter 3
BASIC Equivalents

You can write a large part of your C program using statements that are just like or very similar to BASIC statements. Of course, they have no line numbers, are written with lowercase letters, and end with a semicolon. But they use the same keywords as BASIC statements, and perform the same or nearly the same operations. These are the C language statements that are equivalent to BASIC statements:

1. Assignment statement
2. if statement
3. for loop
4. while loop
5. goto statement

Assignment Statement
The *assignment statement* assigns a value to a variable. The value may be that of a constant, another variable, an expression, or a function. An assignment statement in BASIC is:

100 ITEM = 4875

The C equivalent is:

item = 4875;

Same thing ... almost. BASIC is very secretive about the *type* of a variable. ITEM is automatically assigned single-precision type, and the constant 4875 is assigned integer type. The integer is converted to single precision and stored as a single-precision variable.

C does not assign a type to a variable automatically. The example shown would result in an error message unless it had been preceded by a *declarator*. Chapter 5 contains detailed information about declarators. This declarator assigns type **float** to variable *item*:

float item;

Chapter 3

C's **float** variable is identical to the single-precision variable in BASIC. It is a real number providing six to seven digits of precision. The constant is assigned integer type in C also. It's converted to **float** type and stored as the value of *item*.

The statements are the same in both languages. The difference is that C requires you to declare variables, which shows you at a glance which variables you're using and what type they are. Automatic assignment of types in BASIC sometimes provides strange answers; specific declaration of variables in C puts you in the driver's seat.

C, like some versions of BASIC, includes a type of assignment statement that assigns the same value to more than one variable:

sum1 = sum2 = sum3 = 0;

This statement assigns the value of 0 to variable *sum3* first. Then it assigns the value of *sum3* to variable *sum2*. Last of all, it assigns the value of *sum2* to variable *sum1*. You can use any variable or expression to the right of the rightmost equal sign (instead of the 0).

Here's another example in BASIC:

380 AVE = (VAL1 + VAL2 + VAL3) / 3

The C language statement is:

ave = (val1 + val2 + val3) / 3;

The BASIC statement adds three single-precision values, converts the integer 3 to single precision, and performs single-precision division. The result is stored as a single-precision variable.

Assuming that *val1*, *val2*, *val3*, and *ave* have been declared as **float** type, the C statement provides the same result, but in a different way. A C program performs no **float** type computations. Instead, the program that contains this statement converts *val1*, *val2*, *val3*, and integer 3 to type **double**, and performs the computations. Type **double** is a real-number type that provides 16 to 17 digits of precision. When it's converted and stored, the result is more accurate (potentially, at least) than if the result had been type **float**.

If *val1*, *val2*, and *val3* are declared as integers, you should use a **float** type constant:

ave = (val1 + val2 + val3) / 3.0;

BASIC Equivalents

The program adds the integers, converts the sum and constant to type **double**, performs the computations, and converts the result to **float**. Using 3 instead of 3.0 would have caused all the numbers to be treated as integers, and an integer result would have been converted to **float** and stored. This would probably not be accurate enough.

Here's a more complex BASIC statement that includes a function:

500 SIDE1 = SIN(A) * HYP

The C equivalent is:

side1 = sin(a) * hyp;

The BASIC example calls the SIN function. Some versions of the interpreter return a double-precision result, but most return a single-precision result. The result is a single-precision value in variable SIDE1.

In C, the result is the same, but the computations are **double** type. The function, however, is in one of the libraries that came with your C compiler. The statement causes the compiler to ask the link program to get the function from the library and include it in your program. Chapter 11 contains details about compiling and linking your program. The advantage is that you don't have to use the C compiler or libraries each time you run the program. The library function becomes as much a part of your program as the functions you write and compile.

C assignment statements are very much like BASIC assignment statements. All you need to do is omit the line number, change the letters to lowercase, and add a semicolon.

if Statement

The C **if** statement never needs a "then" and cannot transfer control to another part of the program. It uses parentheses around the relational or logical expression. Otherwise, it is the BASIC IF in lowercase letters and ending with a semicolon. Here's an example in BASIC:

450 IF YEAR MOD 4 THEN FEB = 28 ELSE FEB = 29

In C, you'll need four statements:

```
if (year % 4)
   feb = 28;
else
   feb = 29;
```

Chapter 3

Both versions use modulo division to identify leap years. The percent sign (%) is the modulo division operator in C. When the result is not zero, the variable *feb* is set to 28. When the result is zero, *feb* is set to 29. Like BASIC, C considers a zero value as false and a nonzero value as true. C replaces the BASIC THEN by using parentheses. Whatever comes after the closing parentheses is considered to be the statement to be executed if the expression is true. Now for the bad news. C has no equivalent for this BASIC statement:

500 IF YEAR < 1984 THEN 600 ELSE 650

But the news is really not that bad, because C has a better way to do the same thing. In BASIC, line 600 and lines following are statements to be executed for years prior to 1984. Lines 650 and following are statements that apply to subsequent years. In C, you can put those statements right in the **if** statement:

```
if (year < 1984) {
   rate = .25;
   base = 2500;
   surcharge = .50;
   }
else {
   rate = .26;
   base = 2000;
   surcharge = .52;
   }
```

Whatever it is, it went up in 1984. The important thing to notice is the left brace following the parenthesis. This brace is the beginning of a *compound statement*, or *block*, that is executed for years prior to 1984. The right brace ends the block. All the statements you need for years prior to 1984 go right here instead of somewhere else in your program. Similarly, a block following **else** contains the statements for years 1984 and later—all right here together, where you can't miss them.

In BASIC, you can leave off the ELSE when you don't need it:

400 IF YEAR > 1983 THEN RATE = RATE + .01:BASE = BASE − 500: SURCHARGE = SURCHARGE + .02

You can in C, too:

BASIC Equivalents

```
if (year > 1983) {
   rate = rate + .01;
   base = base - 500;
   surcharge = surcharge + .02;
}
```

You would have to set *rate, base,* and *surcharge* to the values that apply before 1984, or this statement would not give you the same answer. If you set the variables to the 1983 values (with assignment statements), this statement is more efficient in either language. In either version, the statement does nothing if the year is 1983 or earlier.

C's **if** statement works like BASIC's IF statement, and it can make your program more readable by including blocks of statements that otherwise would be in some other part of the program.

for Loop

C's **for** loop is much more versatile than BASIC's FOR-NEXT loop. This section describes the statement that is equivalent to the BASIC statement. Chapter 8 describes the other capabilities of the **for** loop.

The BASIC loop starts with a FOR statement and ends with a NEXT:

```
800 SQ = 1: ODD = 1
810 FOR R = 1 TO 15
820 PRINT SQ, R
830 ODD = ODD + 2
840 SQ = SQ + ODD
850 NEXT R
```

The C loop has no need for NEXT:

```
sq = odd = 1;
for (r = 1; r <= 15; r = r + 1) {
   printf("%d     %d\n",sq, r);
   odd = odd + 2;
   sq = sq + odd;
}
```

Notice that the C statement consists of keyword **for** followed by three expressions enclosed in parentheses and separated by semicolons. The first expression initializes *r*; it corresponds to the FOR R = 1 portion of the BASIC statement. The next expression is evaluated before each repetition of the statements in the loop. This corresponds to the TO 15

Chapter 3

statement. The third expression is executed for each repetition of the loop, after the last statement. This expression corresponds to the STEP 1 option implied in the BASIC statement.

The loop itself is a block, described in the section on the **if** statement. The loop could consist of a single statement. The statements in this block print 15 perfect squares and their roots without multiplying or calling a square root function. How about that?

Whether the loop consists of a single statement or a compound statement (block), no NEXT statement is needed. Either the semicolon that ends the statement or the brace that encloses the block tells the compiler what belongs in the loop.

The **for** statement of C does not look like the FOR statement of BASIC, but **for** statements like the one shown in this section work exactly like BASIC FOR-NEXT loops.

while Loop

The C **while** loop is similar to the WHILE–WEND loop of BASIC. The C version doesn't need the WEND statement for the same reason that the **for** loop does not need a NEXT. Here's an example from BASIC:

```
250 WHILE N <> 21
260 INPUT N
270 N = N + 5
280 WEND
```

The C version is:

```
while (n != 21) {
  scanf("%d",n);
  n = n + 5;
}
```

The **while** keyword is followed by an expression within parentheses. In the example, the expression is a relational one, having a true value (1) or a false value (0). Notice that != means not equal to. The expression could be a numeric expression; in that case, it is considered true when its value is not equal to zero. A zero value is considered false. In either case, the loop is executed as long as the expression is true.

In the C version, the statements of the loop are enclosed in braces and include the **scanf( )** function to accept a decimal number that you type in. The input function is fully described in Chapter 9. These statements are executed until the user

BASIC Equivalents

types 21; then the loop terminates. In either language, it could happen that typing 21 would not get you out of the loop. This would happen if variable n were a real number type and the automatic type conversions introduced a fractional result (21.00001, for example). Declare n as an integer to avoid this problem.

Notice the contrast between **for** and **while** loops. The **for** loop initializes, tests, and increments. The **while** loop only tests. The loop must include some way for the variable to acquire the value required for the test. Otherwise, the loop is repeated until you get tired of it and turn off your computer. Here's the **while** loop version of the **for** loop example:

```
r = sq = odd = 1;
while (r <= 15) {
  printf("%d    %d\n",sq, r);
  odd = odd + 2;
  sq = sq + odd;
  r = r + 1;
}
```

The initialization expression moved to the statement preceding the loop, the incrementing expression moved into the loop, and the keyword changed. Otherwise, the examples are identical.

goto Statement

BASIC's GOTO statement allows you to write unmanageable programs, yet it is unavoidable in many BASIC programs. C's **goto** statement is seldom required. You should avoid using the **goto** statement to keep your programs understandable.

Here's the culprit in BASIC:

400 GOTO 450

In C:

```
goto there;
```

Since C has no line numbers, the **goto** statement has to be different, but it works the same. However, the program must include a statement with "there" as its label:

```
there:year = year + 1; /* You may label any statement */
```

Leave the **goto** statement for use only in dire emergencies.

39

Chapter 3

An Example
You can program solutions for many problems using only the statements described in this chapter, along with input/output functions. Here's an example program you can compile, link, and execute:

```c
#include <stdio.h>
main () /* Balance your checkbook? */
{
double bal, chk, dep;
char in[12];
int c;

printf("Type in statement balance:"); /* Display function */
scanf("%lf", &bal); /* Formatted input function */
printf("Any outstanding deposits? (Y or N) ");
if ((c = getche()) == 'Y') { /* Character input function */
   printf("\nType outstanding deposit: $");
   scanf("%lf", &dep);
   while (dep > 0) {
      bal = bal + dep;
      printf("Type outstanding deposit: $");
      scanf("%lf", &dep);
      }
   }
printf("\nType outstanding check: $");
scanf("%lf", &chk);
while (chk > 0) {
   bal = bal - chk;
   printf("Type outstanding check: $");
   scanf("%lf", &chk);
   }
printf("Your checkbook balance should be $%.2lf",bal);
return;
}
```

Notice the first line of the example. It is a *compiler control line*, required for the input/output statements in the example. The number sign (#) of a compiler control line must be in column 1 of the line, the leftmost character position. For details about compiler control lines, see Chapter 10.

The input/output functions required are **printf( )**, which displays prompting messages on the screen, **scanf( )**, which accepts the numbers you type in, and **getche( )**, which accepts a single character from the keyboard and displays it on the screen. The other executable statements, except **return**, are all

BASIC Equivalents

like BASIC statements. The **return** statement just returns control to MS-DOS.

The program first asks for the balance and stores it after you type it in. Then it asks if there are any outstanding deposits. Using the familiar **if** statement and the character input function, the program accepts the first character you type and requests a deposit amount if you have typed Y. After displaying the prompting message, the program stores the deposit value and enters a **while** loop. Until you type 0 for the deposit amount, the loop is repeated, adding the deposit to the balance and getting another deposit value.

When you type any letter other than Y (and that includes y), the program skips to process the checks, subtracting each check from the previous balance. When you type 0 (for no more checks), the program displays the balance.

One problem with balancing your checkbook is that the computer cannot do a very important part of the job. You have to match the statement to your check record or checkbook stubs, marking the deposits that have been added to your account and the checks that the bank has paid and deducted. Once you have done that, the deposits and checks that have not yet reached the bank (outstanding deposits and checks) are those that remain unmarked in your check record or checkbook stubs. Now you can use your computer. Run the example program. If you have any outstanding deposits, type Y and type them in. Then type in your outstanding checks. The computer tells you how much you have in the bank, assuming that none of the outstanding deposits will bounce and that all of your checks are cashed or deposited.

The program is not very user-friendly, because it skips the processing of deposits if you type any letter but Y. It should at least recognize y. It could reject all letters but Y, y, N, and n, telling you to try again. These refinements use C statements that differ from BASIC; you can add them after you have read a few more chapters.

This program shows that it's possible to program solutions to common problems using only the statements in this chapter. But you can do a lot more with C: things that are done differently from BASIC and things you cannot do in BASIC.

Chapter 4
Functions

Chapter 4
Functions

The C function has some of the characteristics of a BASIC subroutine that is called with a GOSUB statement and returns control to the statement that follows the GOSUB. And like the built-in functions of BASIC, it returns a value, which replaces the name of the function when it is used in an expression. Beyond that, the C function does not resemble anything in BASIC.

This chapter first describes the typical function, one that has one or more arguments and returns a value. Then it describes the function that does not return a value and the function that does not have arguments. Next, it discusses the C language program, the *main( )* function. Last, we'll discuss the library functions that come with your C compiler.

Typical Functions

The typical function performs a specified operation on an *argument* (or arguments) and returns the result of that operation. For example, you might need to know the number of studs required to build a wall or partition. (Studs are the vertical frame members, often two-by-fours, evenly spaced in the framework for a wall or partition.) The arguments are the length of the wall or partition, in feet, and the spacing of the studs, in inches. You could use a function named "studs" with two arguments. Then, in your program, you could call the function like this:

numst = studs(part1, 16);

At this point, you're not concerned with how to figure the number of studs from the length and spacing. Function *studs( )* does that. The arguments are variable *part1* and constant 16, enclosed in parentheses following the function name. You could use a constant, a variable, or an expression for either argument. The first argument must be the length of the wall or partition in feet, and the second must be the number of

Chapter 4

inches between the centers of studs. The statement sets variable *numst* to the number of studs returned by the function.

Now you are ready to write the function:

```
studs(len, sp) /* Computes numbers of studs for wall */
int len, sp;
{
int n;
n = (len * 12)/ sp;
return (n + 1);
}
```

The name of the function and its arguments are written as the first line of the function. It is good practice to place a comment on the first line, enclosed in slashes and asterisks as shown.

Next come the declarators for the arguments and for a variable used in the function. Even though both the arguments and the variable are declared as type **int**, they cannot be declared in one statement. Declarators for arguments must precede the brace ({) that identifies the start of the function proper. Declarators for variables used in the function follow this brace.

After you have declared any variables used by the function, write the executable statements that perform the computations for the function. In the example, a single assignment statement is all you need. It multiplies the length by 12 to get the length in inches and divides by the spacing. This does not allow for a stud at the end of the wall, should the length of the wall not be evenly divisible by the spacing.

The **return** statement consists of the keyword followed by an expression, variable *n* plus one, in parentheses. This expression allows one more stud for the end of the wall. This **return** statement causes your program to provide the value of the expression to the calling statement. And don't forget the closing brace (}) that tells the compiler where the function ends.

This very simple function contains everything that any function needs. First, notice the names of the arguments. They may or may not be the names used in the main program, but they must be the same type. These names are used within the function only. The main program makes a copy of each argument for use in the function. If the function assigned a different value to *len*, the new value would apply only in the

Functions

function, not in the main program. Similarly, the variables declared in the function apply only within the function.

Instead of just one assignment statement to perform the mathematics, you can have as many statements as you need. You can have **if** statements and loops of any kind in your function.

You can have more than one **return** statement in your function. An **if** statement may include a statement to return a different variable when appropriate. But the function can have only one closing brace. The compiler will give a list of error messages if you add extra braces.

A function can return a value of any type. When you don't specify a type, the compiler assumes that the type is *integer*. Often a function returns a *real number*. Consider a program that computes distances in miles and also in kilometers. The function "kilometers" converts miles to kilometers and returns a real number. Among the declarators in the main program, you need to declare the function:

float kilometers( );

To call the function:

kdist = kilometers(mdist);

Variables *kdist* and *mdist* must also be declared **float** type, even though the function is declared.

There's more to declaring the function as type **float**. You must also write the type ahead of the function name as shown in this example which will compile:

```
float kilometers(miles) /* Convert miles to kilometers */
float miles;
{
float n;
n = miles * 1.609344;
return(n);
}
```

One of the beauties of C is that statements can be combined to form very terse code. This function can be reduced to this and will compile:

```
float kilometers(miles) /* Convert miles to kilometers */
float miles;
{
return((float) (miles * 1.609344));
}
```

Chapter 4

The **return** statement can return an expression, a function, or a constant as well as a variable. In this case, the expression that performs the computation of the function is placed in the **return** statement. The **float** in parentheses is called a *cast*. It causes the compiler to convert the result of the multiplication from type **double** to type **float**.

As you design your C program, plan what each function will do, the arguments it will use, and the types of the arguments. Also plan the value to be returned and the type of that value. That is all you need to know to be able to use the function as you write the main program and other functions of the program. Then, when you get to writing the function, declare the arguments and any variables the function needs and write the executable statements. Thus, each function is written and debugged independently of the rest of the program.

Functions That Do Not Return a Value

Not all functions return a value. Some just perform an operation, like displaying a message on the screen. For example, you may want to display the name of a variable and its value during computations. Design a function "display," and give it a string that contains the variable name and the variable itself as arguments. Call the function like this:

```
display(v1name,v1);
```

Only the function name, followed by its arguments in parentheses, is needed to call the function. The function name is used as a statement. Here's the complete function which will compile:

```
display(name, val) /* Display a variable name and value */
char name[ ];
int val;
{
printf"The present value of %s is %d.\n", name, val);
return;
}
```

Type **char** can apply to either a single character or a string of characters. When the variable name includes a pair of braces, **char** refers to a string. In the main program, the string argument contains a specified number of characters. In the function, the number is indefinite; the function can print the string, whether it has more or fewer characters. So no number

Functions

is used between the brackets. The other argument is integer *val*. This function is limited to displaying the values of integers.

The function itself requires no variables. The **printf** statement is not really a statement, but a call to the formatted output function **printf( )**, described in Chapter 9. All the characters within quotation marks are displayed, except %s, %d, and \n. The function inserts the string *name* instead of %s, and the decimal value of *val* instead of %d. Characters \n cause the cursor to go to a new line. If *name* is "feet" and *val* is 25, the computer displays this message on the screen:

The present value of feet is 25.

Notice that the **return** statement has no parentheses; it has nothing to return. You can leave it out entirely if you wish.

The C language function does not necessarily return a value. When it does not, the function is called differently, and the function itself is written differently.

Functions Without Arguments

A function doesn't always have arguments. Or, to be more accurate, the arguments may not need to be specified. For example, you could have a function that would clear the screen on your computer. You could name it "clear" and call it like this:

clear( );

Don't leave the parentheses out when you call a function, even when you have nothing to put between them. Without them, the function name looks like a variable name to the compiler.

Here's a complete function:

```
clear( ) /* Clear the screen */
{
int i;
for (i = 1; i <= 24; i = i + 1)
   putch('\n');
}
```

This function is a lot like the other examples. The output function **putch( )** is new. It is described in Chapter 9. The **for** loop causes the function to be called 24 times, clearing the screen by displaying 24 blank lines. Notice that the function

Chapter 4

doesn't have a **return** statement. You could include one, as in the display function example, for consistency.

main Function

A C program is itself a function called *main( )*. It may or may not have arguments. Ideally, the *main* function performs very little of the processing, but calls other functions corresponding to the major divisions of the program. The example below, if combined with the next four functions, *sum, item, taxcomp,* and *change*, will constitute a complete program that will compile, link, and execute.

```
#include <stdio.h>
#define RATE .05125
main( ) /* Ring up a sale */
{
float total, taxable;
float sum( ), taxcomp( );

total = sum(&taxable);
total = total + taxcomp(taxable);
change(total);
{
```

The first two lines do not look like C statements. As a matter of fact, they are not C, but *compiler control lines*, also called *preprocessor directives*. The number signs (#) that begin compiler control lines must be in the leftmost character positions on the lines. Chapter 10 describes compiler control lines in detail. You saw the first one in a previous example. The second one defines a *symbolic constant* that applies to the entire program. This symbolic constant, RATE, is the sales tax rate in part of Texas. By using a symbolic constant, you have to change only that constant if the sales tax is different where you live. And when the legislature promises not to raise the rate, you can relax, knowing that when they do, you just have one line to change.

The program includes declarators for variables *total* and *taxable* and functions *sum( )* and *taxcomp( )*. These variables and functions are **float** type.

The program consists of two assignment statements, each of which calls a function, and an additional function call. Function *sum( )* accepts item amounts you type in, maintaining a total of all items and also a total of taxable items. The function prints the total, returns the total, and stores the taxable

Functions

total in variable *taxable*. Usually, a function uses a copy of an argument. But when an argument is preceded by an ampersand (**&**), the program passes the address of the argument to the function. The function stores the taxable total in the variable *taxable* using the address. In this way, the function returns two values, one in the usual way, and the other using the address of the variable (*pointer*). Pointers are described in detail in Chapter 6.

Here's function *sum( )*:

```
float sum(ttotal) /* Accept and display items */
float *ttotal;
{
float tot, cost, taxitem, item( );
tot = *ttotal = 0;
printf("Type in the amount of an item. If the item\n");
printf("is taxable, type T. If not, type a space.\n");
printf("Press RETURN. After last item type 0 and a\n");
printf("space. Press RETURN.\n\n");
tot = tot + item(&taxitem);
*ttotal = *ttotal + taxitem;
while ((cost = item(&taxitem)) != 0) {
   tot = tot + cost;
   *ttotal = *ttotal + taxitem;
   }
if (*ttotal > 0)
   printf("Subtotal:              $%.2f\n", tot);
return(tot);
}
```

Notice that the declarator for variable **ttotal* has an asterisk (*****) as its first character. Variable *ttotal* is the argument that consists of an address (pointer). The asterisk in front of the variable name in the called function tells the compiler that this is a pointer.

Function *sum( )* calls function *item( )* to accept each item from the keyboard. Function *item( )* displays a dollar sign and calls the **scanf( )** function to obtain the amount and a character. For a taxable item, type in a T. For other items, type in an additional space. When you type in a T, the function copies the amount into variable *taxitem* in function *sum( )*, using a pointer. When you type in a space (or some other character), the function copies zero into *taxitem*.

51

Chapter 4

Here's function *item( )*:

```
float item(taxamt) /* Get item */
float *taxamt;
{
float amt;
char c;
printf("                      $");
scanf("%f%c", &amt, &c);
if (c == 'T')
   *taxamt = amt;
else
   *taxamt = 0;
return(amt);
}
```

Function *taxcomp( )* computes the tax and displays the amount of tax on the screen. It returns the amount of the tax, and the assignment statement that calls function *taxcomp( )* adds the tax to the total.

Function *taxcomp( )* looks like this:

```
float taxcomp(taxtot) /* Computes sales tax */
float taxtot;
{
float tax;

if (taxtot > 0) {
   tax = taxtot * RATE;
   printf("Sales Tax:            $%.2f\n",tax);
   }
else
   tax = 0;
return(tax);
}
```

Function *change( )* displays the total, accepts the amount tendered, and calculates the change. It also displays the amount tendered and the change. Notice that the type of function *change( )* is not declared. Since function *change( )* does not return a value, the default type, integer, is satisfactory.

Here's function *change( )*:

```
change(gtot) /* Displays total and computes change */
float gtot;
{
float amtt;
```

Functions

```
printf("Total:                    $%.2f\n", gtot);
printf("Amount Tendered: $");
scanf("%f", amtt);
amtt = amtt - gtot;
if (amtt < 0)
   printf("You owe me:            $");
else
   printf("Change:                $");
printf("%.2f\n", abs(amtt));
return;
}
```

Passing Data to a Program

MS-DOS lets you type additional information following a program name when you run a program. The *main()* function can have two arguments that it uses to access this information. One of these arguments tells the program how many strings are available. The other is the address of a string array that contains the strings. For example, you might type this command line to run a program:

convert 250

Or you might type this to run the same program:

convert 0x20D

The program below consisting of the next five functions, *main, hdconv, atob, dhconv,* and *atou,* will compile, link, and run. The program will get the number you typed after the program name (convert) and do different things according to what you typed. If you type the program name and a decimal number from 0 to 65535, it will convert it to hexadecimal. Typing the program name followed by a hexadecimal number between 0 and FFFF, in C format (0xFF, for example), will be converted to a decimal number.

The *main* function looks like this:

```
#include <stdio.h>
main(n,parstr) /* Convert decimal numbers to hexadecimal */
int n;         /* and vice versa */
char *parstr[ ];
{
if (n != 2) {
   printf("Try again. I need a number to convert!\n");
   return;
   }
```

Chapter 4

```
printf("%s converts to ",parstr[1])
if (parstr[1][1] == 'x')
   hdconv(parstr[1]);
else
   dhconv(parstr[1]);
return;
}
```

The argument names in this example are not those you find in C books; the conventional names for *n* and *parstr* are *argc* and *argv*, respectively. You can use any variable names acceptable to C compilers. Whatever you call them, the integer variable is always greater than zero, and the string array always contains at least one string. In C programs on some computers, the string corresponding to *parstr[0]* contains the program name. MS-DOS keeps the name of the program a secret; when you use C with MS-DOS, the string corresponding to *parstr[0]* contains a single character: *c*.

The first **if** statement compares the number of arguments to 2, and prints a message and returns to MS-DOS when there is only one or more than two arguments. The second **if** statement looks for an *x* in the string, and calls function *hdconv( )* when *x* is present. When *x* is not present, the statement calls function *dhconv( )*. The **return** statement returns to MS-DOS. Function *hdconv( )* performs hexadecimal to decimal conversion:

```
hdconv(num) /* Convert num to a decimal integer */
char num[ ];
{
int i;
unsigned s;

i = 2;
s = atob(num[i],16);
while (num[++i] != '\0') {
   s = s * 16;
   s = s + atob(num[i],16);
   }
printf("%u\n",s);
return;
}
```

The function calls function *atob( )* to convert each ASCII character to the equivalent binary number. It places the binary number derived from the first character in variable *s* and loops through two statements until all characters in the string have

Functions

been processed. Each time through the loop, variable s is multiplied by 16, and the binary equivalent of the next character is added to the product. The result is the binary equivalent of the hexadecimal number you typed in.

Here's function *atob( )*:

```
atob(c,b)  /* Convert ASCII to binary */
char c;    /* Hexadecimal or decimal */
int b;
{
int n;
if (c >= '0' && c <= '9')
   n = c - '\x30';
else if (c >= 'A' && c <= 'F' && b == 16)
   n = c - '\x37';
  else if (b == 10) {
     printf("\nCharacters 0 - 9 only\n");
     exit( );
     }
  else {
     printf("Characters 0 - 9");
     printf("and A - F only\n");
     exit( );
     }
return (n);
}
```

Function *atob( )* converts ASCII codes to binary values. It accepts ASCII codes of either hexadecimal digits or decimal digits, according to the value of the second argument, *b*. First, the function subtracts hexadecimal 30 from the ASCII codes for numbers 0–9. Look in Appendix C at the ASCII codes, and notice that for these digits, the remainder from this subtraction is the binary value of the digit. For hexadecimal digits A–F, the function subtracts hexadecimal 37 from the ASCII code, which also yields the binary value. For other characters, the function prints an error message and exits. Notice that the function rejects digits A–F unless argument *b* is equal to 16.

Function *dhconv( )* converts decimal numbers to hexadecimal values. The function looks like this:

```
dhconv(num) /* Converts a decimal number to hexadecimal */
char num[ ];
{
static char htab[ ] = {'0','1','2','3','4','5','6','7','8', '9','A','B','C',
       'D','E','F'};
```

55

Chapter 4

```
int i, n[4];
char c;
unsigned x, atou( );
x = atou(num);
for (i = 0; i < 4; i++) {
  n[i] = x % 16;
  x = x / 16;
  }
printf("0x");
for (i = 3; i >= 0; i--) {
  c = htab[n[i]];
  putchar(c);
  }
putchar['\n'];
return;
}
```

    The fourth line of the function introduces two new concepts. First, character array *htab* is storage class **static**. Storage classes are described in detail in Chapter 5. This array has to be a static array because it has to be assigned values. The other concept is *initialization*, the assignment of values to the elements of the array. Array *htab* consists of 16 elements, each of which contains the ASCII character that corresponds to the number of the element. That is, element 0 contains ASCII 0; element 1, ASCII 1; element 10, ASCII A; and element 15, ASCII F. This array is a *translation table* used to print hexadecimal digits correctly.

    The function calls function *atou( )* to convert an ASCII character string to an unsigned number, variable x. Next, it enters a loop computing a hexadecimal digit each time through the loop. The first statement of the loop computes the digit by dividing variable x by 16 and storing the remainder in array n. The second statement sets x to the quotient resulting from dividing x by 16. After the loop has been repeated four times, the binary values corresponding to the four hexadecimal digits are in the elements of array n.

    The second loop in the function uses translation table *htab* to convert the binary values to ASCII characters and displays the characters. The function closes by performing a new line operation.

    Function *atou( )* returns an unsigned number equivalent to the ASCII characters in a string:

Functions

```
unsigned atou(num) /* Converts string to unsigned */
char num[ ];
{
unsigned n;
int i;
i = 0;
n = atob(num[i],10);
while (num[++i] != '\0') {
   n = n * 10;
   n = n + atob(num[i],10);
   }
return (n);
}
```

Notice keyword **unsigned** just ahead of the function name on the first line of function *atou( )*. This is required because the function returns an unsigned value. Function *atou( )* calls function *atob( )* to convert each ASCII character in string *num* to its binary value. Notice that the second argument is 10. This causes function *atob( )* to reject ASCII characters other than 0 through 9. The function stores the binary value of the first digit in unsigned variable *n*. Then, for each digit in the string, the function multiplies the variable by 10 and adds the binary value of the digit. The function returns variable *n* when the last digit has been processed.

This program shows you how to access an argument that you type following the program name when you run a program. In addition, it performs a useful function: converting decimal numbers to hexadecimal and hexadecimal numbers to decimal. Appendix B describes hexadecimal numbers and tells how to convert them to decimal numbers. If you are not familiar with hexadecimal numbers, you should study Appendix B. In the meantime, you've got a program to do the work for you. You can type in numbers as large as you please; the program gives correct results only for decimal numbers 0–65535 and hexadecimal numbers 0–FFFF.

Library Functions

If you have the Lattice C Compiler, you have a variety of library functions. The other C compilers also come with libraries of functions. A *library function* is a function that the developer of your compiler has written for you to use in your programs. You can call it just as you call the functions you

Chapter 4

write. The manual that comes with your compiler tells you what the arguments are for each function and how to call it. When you link the program, be sure to include the library that contains the function, as described in Chapter 11.

Calls to many of the functions from the library are automatically placed in the object code without your having to call them specifically. Functions that perform arithmetic operations with **double** type numbers and those that convert numbers of one type to another type are called automatically. The compiler does all the work, inserting the call and the arguments for you. The input/output functions are also library functions. Typical input/output functions are described fully in Chapter 9. Other library functions perform the transcendental functions of trigonometry and the logarithmic and exponential functions of algebra. Still others perform memory management functions, string functions, conversion functions, and random number generation. The library of C language functions supplied with the Lattice C Compiler includes many functions that you need from time to time. They simplify the programming effort.

Functions are the building blocks of a C language program. Define each function in terms of what it does and what arguments and other data items it needs. Then write executable statements to do the job. That's all there is to C programming.

Chapter 5
Declarators

Chapter 5
Declarators

A major difference between BASIC and C is that C requires all data to be declared. BASIC doesn't require anything similar to declaring a data item, except for arrays with greater than ten elements. In that case, BASIC requires a DIM statement.

This chapter describes the *declarators* for each data type and for structures, fields, and unions. It describes the structures, fields, and unions themselves, and it also describes *storage classes*, which are related to data types, but are different, and the *scope* of each storage class.

Integers

Use keyword **int** to declare an integer variable:

int one, two, three;

This example declares three integer variables: *one*, *two*, and *three*. The declarator tells the compiler that these items each require two bytes of memory (under MS-DOS), and that values assigned to these variables must be converted to integer type unless they are already integer type. The contents of these items are evaluated as signed integers in the range of −32,768 through 32,767.

You can use the declarator statement to initialize the value of a variable:

int mile = 5280;

This example declares variable *mile* and assigns the value 5280 to the variable.

Type **long int** is a data type that is not available in BASIC. It is a 32-bit integer (under MS-DOS), also called a double-precision integer. The range of values is −2,147,483,648 through 2,147,483,647—not enough digits for the national debt, but enough for many calculations. You'll get greater accuracy using double-precision integers than if integers are entered as floating-point numbers. The declarator statement is:

long int vel;

Chapter 5

This statement tells the compiler to reserve four bytes for variable *vel*, to convert any value assigned to the variable to **long** integer type, and to insert calls to **long** integer arithmetic functions when computations with the variable are required.

To declare a variable as an unsigned integer, use keyword **unsigned**:

unsigned num;

This example declares variable *num* as an **unsigned** integer. An **unsigned** integer is assumed to be positive; the range of values is 0 to 65,535 (under MS-DOS). The compiler reserves two bytes of memory for the variable and generates the appropriate code for arithmetic operations.

The short integer is the same size as the integer in the MS-DOS implementation of Lattice C. The range of values is $-32{,}768$ to $32{,}767$. The declarator for a short integer is:

short small;

You can use short integer variables in your program even though they are no different from integer variables. However, in some computers short integers are different. The use of the **short** type is important only when your program might be used on a computer in which short integers are not the same as integers.

Floating-Point Numbers

Use keyword **float** to declare a single-precision floating-point variable:

float rate;

Values range from $\pm 1.0 * 10^{-37}$ through $\pm 1.0 * 10^{38}$ (under MS-DOS). These variables occupy four bytes of memory. The compiler automatically calls functions to convert these numbers to type **double** before performing any calculations. It calls functions to convert the result to type **float** before assigning it to a single-precision variable.

Declare a double-precision floating-point variable like this:

double assets;

You can use keywords **long float** instead of **double** if you prefer. The range of values is $\pm 1.0 * 10^{-307}$ through $\pm 1.0 * 10^{308}$ (under MS-DOS). The Lattice C Compiler converts all floating-point numbers used in computations to type **double** and performs all arithmetic in double precision.

Declarators

Characters and Strings
Character type variables are declared this way:

char letter;

You can initialize the variable with the declarator statement:

char letter = 'd';

A group of characters is a string, declared like this:

char name[10];

This statement reserves space for ten characters, which is ten bytes (under MS-DOS). The usual way to initialize a string in a declarator is:

char title[ ] = "Yankee Doodle";

This is a special case of initialization. In C, a string is an array of characters followed by a null (0) character. But in the example, the number of characters is not specified (you could, if you like to count). The compiler adds the null character to "Yankee Doodle" and counts the total number of characters to obtain the number that would otherwise go between the brackets.

Special Data Structures
It's often convenient to group a set of data items together in a logical organization of the data. For example, a personnel record might contain a name, an address, an employee number, a salary amount, and an earnings-to-date amount. The name and address are strings, while the other items are numeric values. BASIC has no real solution to the problem of arranging this data for efficient processing. You could define a string array:

100 DIM EMP$(100,5)

This would provide five strings of data for each of 100 employees. You could access the name of the first employee with EMP$(0,0), the address with EMP$(0,1), the employee number with EMP$(0,2), the salary with EMP$(0,3), and the earnings with EMP$(0,4). But if you want to do any computations with the numbers, you have to convert the strings to numbers.

Chapter 5

Another way is to use two closely related arrays, one for the strings and one for the numbers:

100 DIM EMP$(100,2), EMP(100,3)

This allows you to access the name and address for the first employee as EMP$(0,0) and EMP$(0,1), respectively. Use EMP(0,0), EMP(0,1), and EMP(0,2) to access the employee number, salary, and earnings. This solves the problem of type conversion, but it is not a really good solution.

C has a better solution: the *structure* data type. A structure can contain the data items that apply to an entity; each data item can be of any type available in the language. Here's the declarator statement for the personnel record:

```
struct pers {
   char name[20];
   char address[20];
   int empno;
   float salary;
   float earnings;
};
```

This example declares a *pers* structure that consists of two strings, an integer, and two floating-point numbers. The *pers* refers to the structure organization (or template), not to a location in memory that contains these items. To reserve memory for an actual structure, add the name of a structure to the declaration:

struct pers emp;

Once you have declared data structure *pers*, you can declare additional structures without repeating the list of data items. This example provides a structure for the information that applies to an employee. The name of the structure is *emp*. You can access the name of the employee as *emp.name*. The other data items for the employee are *emp.address, emp.empno, emp.salary,* and *emp.earnings*. An array of *pers* structures is the equivalent of the BASIC array EMP$ except that each data item for an employee has the appropriate data type and a meaningful identifier.

You can also initialize the values. Here's an example:

struct pers newemp = {"Jim Smith","307 W. Center St.", 7230,2500.00,10000.00};

This declarator statement reserves memory for a *pers* structure. The names you use to access data in this structure

Declarators

are *newemp.name, newemp.address, newemp.empno, newemp.salary,* and *newemp.earnings.*

Notice that these examples use a tag for the structure. This refers to the template, not to the actual data locations. Use a tag wherever you need to define more than one structure that uses the same template. You can omit the tag when you do not need it.

You cannot move a structure; you can only move items of a structure, or a *pointer* to a structure. Since a pointer consists of two bytes (under MS-DOS), while a structure may contain many bytes, moving the pointer is much more efficient. Pointers are pretty much the same, whether they point to structures or arrays.

You will often declare an array of structures rather than a single structure. Chapter 6, which describes arrays and pointers, contains an example of a program that uses an array of structures.

C provides a special structure that allows you to access a single bit or group of bits of an unsigned integer. In this way, an unsigned integer can represent as many as 16 items that can have either of two values: 0 (false) or 1 (true). The personnel record of the structure example could use an unsigned integer to contain lots of essential information. For example, an employee may be temporary or permanent, part-time or full-time, hourly or salaried, a manager or individual contributor, or an apprentice or journeyman. All of this information can be stored in a single unsigned integer instead of using many bytes for Y or N characters. To define a structure that assigns names to bits, use this declarator statement:

```
struct {
   unsigned permanent  : 1;
   unsigned full-time  : 1;
   unsigned salaried   : 1;
   unsigned managerial : 1;
   unsigned apprentice : 1;
   unsigned journeyman : 1;
} status;
```

This declarator could be added to the declarator statement of the *pers* structure. Whether part of a larger structure or separate, this structure consists of six *fields*. Each of the fields consists of a single bit. A field can be a group of adjacent bits,

Chapter 5

where appropriate. When the fields of a structure occupy more bits than an unsigned integer contains, the structure uses two (or more) adjacent unsigned integers. A field is not split between two integers; if the current integer does not have enough bits for the field, the compiler assigns the field in the next integer, leaving the unused bits of the current integer vacant.

To access the first bit in this structure, when this structure is part of structure *emp*, use this name: *emp.status.permanent*. You can test its value or set it to either zero or one. In BASIC, you would use a *mask* and the AND operation to test the value of a bit or a mask and an OR operation to set a bit. You could do that in C, too, but C provides the field structure for this purpose.

Another structure that C provides is the **union**. Like other structures, it holds several data items, usually of different types. Unlike other structures, it holds only one of these data items at once. Your program must keep track of the type of the data item currently occupying the **union**. The declarator statement for a **union** is:

```
union num {
   int whole;
   long int big;
   float real;
} number;
```

The compiler reserves enough memory space for type **long int** or **float**, both of which require four bytes (under MS-DOS). When the program has an integer to store, it uses identifier *number.whole*. Similarly, it uses *number.big* for a long integer and *number.real* for a floating-point value. If more than one of the numbers that you might put in a **union** must be available at any one time, you can put only one of the contending numbers in the **union**.

A **union** can sometimes save memory space, but you won't use it often.

Chapter 4 includes a program for converting numbers as an example of a *main()* function that obtains an argument from the MS-DOS command line. The program calls function *dhconv()* to convert a decimal number to hexadecimal. As an example of the use of fields and a **union**, here is an alternative *dhconv()* function:

Declarators

```c
#include <stdio.h>
dhconv(num) /* Converts a decimal number to hexadecimal */
char num[ ];
{
unsigned atou( );
union hexu {
  unsigned numb;
  struct {
    unsigned digit1 :4;
    unsigned digit2 :4;
    unsigned digit3 :4;
    unsigned digit4 :4;
  } deci;
} hex;

hex.numb = atou(num);
printf("0x");
puthex(hex.deci.digit1);
puthex(hex.deci.digit2);
puthex(hex.deci.digit3);
puthex(hex.deci.digit4);
printf("\n");
return;
}
```

Notice the declarator statement that declares **union** *hex*, which has *hexu* for its tag. The **union** contains two members: unsigned integer *numb* and structure *deci*. The first executable statement of the function assigns the value returned by function *atou( )* to *hex.numb*. This value is the binary equivalent of the number you type in following the program name.

Separating the bits of a binary number into groups of four bits and converting each group of four bits into a hexadecimal digit is another way of converting a number to hexadecimal. Structure *deci* divides the 16-bit value in **union** *hex* into four four-bit fields. This is actually a sneaky way to perform division by 16. The function calls function *puthex( )* to display these values as hexadecimal digits. Function *puthex( )* follows:

```c
puthex (digit) /* Displays hexadecimal digit */
unsigned digit;
{
static char htab[ ] = {'0','1','2','3','4','5','6','7','8','9','A','B','C',
        'D','E','F'};
char c;
```

Chapter 5

```
c = htab[digit];
printf("%c",c);
return;
}
```

The executable portion of function *puthex( )* is very similar to the last **for** loop in the *dhconv( )* function in Chapter 4. It uses the argument, an unsigned integer, as the subscript of translation table *htab*, and assigns the value from the table to character *c*. Then it calls function *printf( )* to display the character.

If you like this version of function *dhconv( )* better than the one in Chapter 4, you can substitute the statements of these two functions for those of the other version in the source file. Then compile and link the source file. If you do this, omit the **#include** directive on the first line. Or you can type the new functions on a separate source file and compile it. Then delete (or mark as a comment) the statements of function *dhconv( )* in the original source file and recompile it. Link the two object files as described in Chapter 11. The second method combines the functions at the object code level; this takes more time, but provides a function that you can link with other programs.

Storage Classes

In C, any type of variable can be stored as a variable of any storage class. The *storage class* of a variable determines where memory space for the variable is assigned, that is, where it is stored. You probably think that you could care less, but where a data item is stored determines whether or not it is available to a function of the program. That is, where memory space is assigned for a variable determines the *scope* of the variable. So you really do care.

By having variables available only in some parts of the program, you're protected from errors caused when a statement in some other part of the program alters the value of a variable. Most BASIC programmers have, at some time or other, used the same name for two different variables in different parts of the program. That's good for a surprise or two, particularly when you seldom execute one of the two parts of the program.

Declarators

External storage class. The storage class with the greatest scope is the *external* storage class. Those data items that you declare outside any function (that is, ahead of the first function or between functions) are external. These data items can be made available to the entire program. You can use the declarator statement to initialize all types of external data.

The initial declarator statement for an external data item *defines* the item, which means that it causes the compiler to reserve memory space for the item. In the source file in which an item is defined, all functions that follow the definition can access the data item. If a function ahead of the definition needs to access the item, that function must have a declarator statement for the data item. This declarator differs from the one that defines the item; it has the keyword **extern** ahead of the type keyword in the declarator statement.

When a program has more than one source file, only one of the source files can contain the definition of an external data item. The other source files that contain functions that access the data item must have a declarator with keyword **extern** ahead of the first function that uses the item. The declarator makes the data item available; the keyword tells the compiler not to reserve memory space for it.

Figure 5-1 is a program consisting of two source files. A declarator that defines variable *count* and initializes it to zero is placed immediately ahead of function *display( )*. In order for the first function, *main( )*, to be able to use the variable, function *main( )* also has a declarator for *count*. The second source file also contains a declarator for *count*, making it available to the functions in that file. Variable *count* has a scope that includes the entire program.

The address of a data item or instruction in a program that runs in the 8086/8088 microprocessor has two parts: a segment address and an offset. The segment address is placed in a *segment register* and applies to many data items or instructions. A segment consists of those data items or instructions that are addressed using that segment register. The offsets for the data items or instructions are calculated for the segment address in that segment register. External data items are addressed using the Data Segment (DS) register; to put it another way, they are in the data segment.

Chapter 5

Figure 5-1. External Storage Class Example
Source File One

```
main( ) /* A do-nothing program that shows externals */
{
extern int count; /* Declares count for main */
   .
   . Additional declarators and executable statements
   .
}        /* End of main function */
         .  A function placed at this point in the file
         .  would not have access to variable count
         .  without an extern declaration
int count = 0;   /* Defines variable count */
display (str)    /* Displays a string on the screen */
char str[ ];     /* Count is available to this function */
{
   .
   . Declarators and executable statements
   .
}
```

Source File Two

```
extern int count; /* Declares count for file two */
   .
   . Additional functions
   .
```

Static storage class. The storage class having the next smaller scope is the *static* storage class. This class is subdivided into the external static class and the internal static class. In this case, external means outside a function, and internal means inside a function. Lattice C treats external static data items exactly like external data items. Other versions of C recognize a difference between the two. The difference is that external static data items are available only in the source file in which they are declared, and only to functions that follow the declarator statement in the source file. Keyword **static** must precede the type keyword in the declarator statement.

Figure 5-2 is an example of an external static data item in a source file. The integer *index* is required only in functions *get( )* and *store( )*. Placing the declarator just ahead of these functions makes the variable available only to them. Remem-

Declarators

ber that if you are using Lattice C, you can make *index* available in function *main( )* with an **extern int index;** declarator. You can make the variable available to functions in another source file by using the same declarator in that file.

Figure 5-2. External Static Declarator Example

```
main ( ) /* A do-nothing program that shows a static item */
{
    .
    . Declarators and executable statements
    .
}
    .
    . Additional functions
    .
static int index; /* Declares index for rest of file */
get( ) /* Do-nothing function */
{
    .
    . Declarators and executable statements
    .
}
store( ) /* Do-nothing function */
{
    .
    . Declarators and executable statements
    .
}
```

    An internal static data item is declared within a function; the function is the scope of the data item. The purpose of a static data item inside a function is to provide a data item that passes from one activation of the function to the next. That is, the value in an internal static variable when it returns to the calling function is still there the next time the function is called. An internal static variable is a means of passing a value to the next activation of a function. The compiler reserves memory space for both internal and external data items in the data segment.
    A very important use for an internal static data item is for a string or structure that has an initial value. You can use the declarator statement to initialize the value of any static data item.

Chapter 5

Formal arguments. Although not a storage class, the *formal arguments* of functions have characteristics that you need to be aware of. The formal arguments are written within parentheses immediately following the function name on the first line of a function. Declarators for these arguments immediately follow the first line. They are used to represent the actual arguments that are passed to the function when it is called.

The declarator statements for the formal arguments tell the compiler the types of the arguments. No storage class keyword is needed, and the declarators do not reserve any memory space. The scope of a formal argument is the function in which it is declared. The automatic storage class data items are also declared within functions. Any declarator within a function that either has no storage class keyword or has the storage class keyword **auto** declares an automatic data item. Like the formal arguments, automatic data items are available only within the function in which they are declared, and they do not remain for the next activation of the function. You can use the declarator statement to initialize the values of numeric automatic data items (integers and real numbers). You cannot initialize the values of automatic arrays and structures using the declarator statement.

The scope of an automatic data item extends only from the declarator statement to the right brace matching the left brace that precedes the declaration. When you declare a data item at the beginning of the function, the scope of the data item is the entire function. But you can place a declaration within a compound statement or block (two or more statements enclosed in braces used in an **if**, **while**, **do**, or **for** statement). In that case, the scope of the data item is the block. You do not often want to do this, but it works when you need it.

Automatic data items are stored on the stack. The *stack* is a set of memory locations, somewhat like the discard pile in some rummy games. You put your card on top of the pile, and the next player has to take the top card first. Like the discard pile, the size of the stack is dynamic and the last item in is the first item out. The 8086/8088 microprocessor uses a stack to store data temporarily; C programs that run in this microprocessor use this same stack for automatic data items.

Figure 5-3 shows the internal declarators for function *help( )*. Formal argument *string* is declared first. Notice that the

Declarators

declarator does not specify the length of the string. The compiler needs to know only that it is a string. It can have a different length during each activation. Next is static integer *count*, declared static to allow it to count activations of the function. Integer *num* is an automatic variable available to the entire function. A **for** statement contains a block of statements that include a declarator statement. This statement declares character variable *c*, the scope of which is limited to the block within the **for** statement. Of course, no function would have this combination of declarators, but each of them is typical of statements you can use in your functions.

Figure 5-3. Example of Declarators in a Function

```
help(string) /* Do-nothing function example */
char string[ ];
{                    /* Start of function */
static int count;    /* Initialized to zero by the compiler */
int num;             /* Valid only during one activation */
  .
  . Executable statements
  .
for (.....) { /* Start of block */
  char c;
  .
  . Executable statements
  .
  } /* End of block */
} /* End of function */
```

The Lattice C Compiler for the 8086/8088 microprocessor-based computers stores *register* storage class variables as if they were automatic variables. Register variables are stored in registers in some computers, although the compiler always reserves the right to store them as automatic variables when all registers are being used. A register data item must have the storage class keyword **register** in its declarator statement.

A *register* is a temporary storage device that is accessed more quickly than a memory location. A microprocessor that computes 16-bit numbers (like the 8086/8088) has registers that store 16-bit *words* and 8-bit *bytes* to be used in the computation and for storing results. Since the 8086/8088 microprocessor has only eight general registers, the possibility of

Chapter 5

having a register available for a register data item is not very great. That is, most of the time most of the registers are being used. So the Lattice C Compiler puts register data items on the stack as automatic data items. You should use the register data type in programs that might be transported to computers that use register variables.

This chapter described the declarator statements for all data types and all storage classes. It discussed the storage classes and the purpose for each. While having to declare data items may seem more difficult than just using them, as you do in BASIC, it pays off when you are looking for a bug. Not only that, but declaring data items makes modular programming possible.

Chapter 6

Arrays and Pointers

Chapter 6
Arrays and Pointers

The C *array* is like the familiar array of BASIC. Like BASIC, C allows an array of any data type; it just has more data types. BASIC has nothing even similar to the C pointer. A *pointer* is an address of a data item, an array, or a structure member.

This chapter begins by telling you about arrays; then it tells you about pointers. It also gives you an idea of the power and efficiency of using pointers to manipulate array members. Doesn't sound too difficult, does it? It's not, when you take it one step at a time.

Arrays

The first member of a C array is element 0. If you choose to ignore element 0, it remains unused. Unlike in BASIC, you don't have the option provided by the OPTION BASE statement of starting with either 0 or 1. And there is another subtle difference.

The BASIC DIM statement for an array consisting of elements 0-5, with no OPTION BASE statement in the program, is:

100 DIM AR(5)

Array AR has six elements, with a dimension of 5. The same array in C is declared like this:

float ar[6];

The number in brackets provides a six-element array. The elements are numbered 0 through 5. This is more logical than the BASIC statement, but if you are accustomed to using the maximum dimension in a BASIC DIM statement, you'll have to change your habits.

The DIM statement for a three-dimensional array in BASIC is:

110 DIM NUM (5,4,9)

Chapter 6

That provides 300 single-precision elements when no OPTION BASE statement applies. A similar array is declared in C like this:

float num[6][5][10];

Here, each dimension is enclosed in its own set of brackets. The statement declares 6 arrays of five elements, each of which is an array of ten elements. The difference is not important when you access a single element as you do in BASIC. But since the declaration also means 6 two-dimensional arrays or 30 single-dimensioned arrays, you can access any of these subarrays as if it were not part of the three-dimensional array. That is, you can process any of the 6 two-dimensioned arrays independently of the rest of array *num*. Or you can use any of the 30 single-dimensioned arrays as if it were a separate array.

For instance, if you have a function that processes a single-dimensioned array of type **float**, you can use *num[0][0]* as an argument in the function call. This argument passes the address of the first element of the first ten-element subarray to the function. The function processes this subarray without knowing or caring that there are 29 others where it came from.

Strings

In C, a string is an array of characters. To assign a string to a variable in BASIC, use a statement like this:

480 S$ = "United States"

String variable S$ can be assigned any number of characters within the limit of the maximum-length string. In C, you can declare string *s* with an initial value of "United States":

static char s[ ] = "United States";

This looks like an array of 13 characters, right? Wrong. It's a 14-character string. The extra character is the null character that marks the end of the string, written ' \0'; it is a byte having a zero value (all bits set to zero). When the compiler reads a declarator statement that contains a string constant, it adds a null character at the end of the string. The I/O functions that read strings and the string manipulation functions in the library also supply the null character.

Not every array of characters is a string. You can declare a character array that is not a string:

static char c[ ] = {'A','B','C','D','F'};

Arrays and Pointers

Array *c* is an array of five characters; the last character in the array is 'F', not '\0'. This is a character array, not a string. If used as a string, the results are unpredictable. The program would extend the string to the first zero-value byte. You could get some real surprises if you try to print this array as a string.

Strings can be a real booby trap for BASIC programmers. Resist all temptation to try this:

s = "United States"; /* WRONG! */

Even if *s* is defined as a character array of 14 or more characters, you will get an error every time.

You can't assign a string because a string is an array; assigning an array means moving each element of the array individually. The library contains a function that does it for you:

strcpy (s,"United States");

On the other hand, you can address each character in the string individually:

if (s[5] == 'd')
　s[5] ='\0';

This **if** statement truncates "United States" to "Unite", but leaves the string unaltered if *s* contains "Texas" or "Louisiana".

Structure Arrays

The really powerful array is the array of structures. Analyze this declarator statement:

```
struct {
  char name[20];
  char major[10];
  float gpa;
  struct {
    unsigned dorm    : 1;
    unsigned senior  : 1;
    unsigned jun     : 1;
    unsigned soph    : 1;
    unsigned fresh   : 1;
    } flags;
  } student[50];
```

This statement declares an array of 50 structures. Each structure contains two strings, a real number, and a structure of fields. The structure of fields contains a set of flags, which identify resident students and indicate how far their education

Chapter 6

has progressed. To access the data items for the first student, use *student[0].name* for the name, *student[0].major* for the student's major, and *student[0].gpa* for the grade point average. Use *student[0].flags.dorm, student[0].flags.senior, student[0].flags.jun, student[0].flags.soph,* and *student[0].flags.fresh* to access the flags individually.

Pointers

A *pointer* is the address of a data item. That's a very concise and accurate definition, but it doesn't begin to tell what you can do with pointers. When you want to move an integer or its pointer, you have two bytes to move; you may as well move one as the other. But when you have a type **double** data item to move, that requires moving eight bytes; it's easier to move the two-byte pointer. And when you have an array or structure, moving the pointer instead of the item is a great deal easier. For a long time, programmers have used the technique of moving addresses of data rather than the data itself with good results. C has the capability built in.

Pointers to numeric variables. Unless you use a pointer as an argument, the function has its own copy of an argument to do with as it likes. Programmers call this a *call by value* argument. Using a pointer as the argument of a function is required whenever the function has to alter the data element addressed by the pointer. For example, a function can have more than one result to return to the calling function. The **return** statement can return only one value. Using a pointer for the argument, the function can set the argument to a new value and return another value besides. An argument that is a pointer to the actual argument is called a *call by reference* argument.

Here's an assignment statement that assigns to an integer the value returned by a function:

hrs = time(&min);

Variables *hrs* and *min* have been declared as integers, and variable *min* contains some number of minutes that need to be converted to a number of hours and a number of minutes. The ampersand (**&**) tells the compiler to supply the address of integer *min* as the argument to function *time( )*. That is, an ampersand with the name of a data item identifies a pointer to the data item. It helps if you read *&min* as "the address of *min.*"

Arrays and Pointers

Of course, the function has to know that it is getting a pointer instead of an integer and that the pointer is a pointer to an integer. Here's how:

```
time(num) /* Converts a number of minutes to a */
int *num;  /* number of hours and a number of */
{          /* minutes */
int quo;

quo = *num / 60;
*num = *num % 60;
return (quo);
}
```

The asterisk (*) tells the compiler that *num* is a pointer. You can read *int *num;* as if it were "the contents of *num* is an integer." Similarly, each time **num* is used in an assignment statement, mentally substitute "the contents of *num*." This function uses the address of the argument to access the argument, divide it by 60, and set integer *quo* to the result. Then it uses the address of the argument to access the argument, divide it by 60, and set the argument to the remainder. Argument *min* in the calling function now contains the number of minutes left over after computing the number of hours. The number of hours is in variable *quo*, which function *time( )* returns to the calling function.

You can use a pointer in other ways, too. A pointer doesn't have to be a formal argument. Pointers can be declared among the variables of a function:

```
int *pnum;
```

When a pointer is a formal argument, it is automatically assigned a pointer value. In this case, pointer *pnum* is not automatically assigned the address of an integer. It does not have a value yet. Here's an assignment statement to assign an address to a pointer:

```
pnum = &num;
```

The addition of the letter *p* to the name of a variable is a handy way to get a name for a pointer, but it is the *declarator* that identifies *pnum* as a pointer. The name can be anything.

It's very easy to confuse the symbols used to identify pointers. Both the ampersand (&) and the asterisk (*) are used with pointers. The ampersand tells the compiler to supply an address. The rules are:

81

Chapter 6

1. A name preceded by an **&** is a constant (an address).
2. Use this notation as an argument in a function call.
3. Use this notation to the right of the equal sign in an expression.

The asterisk preceding a name tells the compiler that the name is the name of a pointer. Its rules are:

1. A pointer name preceded by an * is a variable. Its value is the contents of the pointer.
2. Use this notation when you declare a pointer.
3. Use this notation in an assignment statement on either side of the equal sign.

A pointer with no operator ahead of it is a two-byte variable containing an address. Use it on either side of the equal sign in an assignment statement or as an argument in a function call (assuming it has been assigned the proper address value).

Pointers to strings. Now that you have that straight, there is an important exception. Pointers to strings don't need symbols to identify them as pointers, because the name of a string is always a pointer. As an example, here's an old friend from BASIC:

750 A$ = MID$(NAM$,ST,N)

In case you've forgotten, that statement sets string A$ to a substring of NAM$ consisting of N characters starting with character ST. Once you have declared the variables appropriately, you can use this statement to call a C function to do the same thing:

mid(a,nam,st,n);

The function is:

```
mid(str2, str1, start, num) /* Select a substring */
char str2[ ], str1[ ];
int start, num;
{
int i = 0, j;

start = start - 1;
j = start + num;
while (start < j) {
   str2[i] = str1[start];
   i = i + 1;
```

Arrays and Pointers

```
    start = start + 1;
    }
str2[i] = '\0';
return;
}
```

Of course, this function is oversimplified. Argument *st* must be less than the number of characters in argument *nam;* the sum of arguments *st* and *n* must also be less than that number. Additional statements should be added to provide the correct results when other argument values are used. But, as it is, the function shows that string names are actually pointers.

The function does not copy string *nam* into formal argument *str1*. It doesn't copy string *str2* into string *a* either. That could eat up a lot of memory. Instead, arguments *a* and *nam* and formal arguments *str2* and *str1* are pointers. String *a* is built from string *nam* (both strings in the calling function) as function *mid( )* runs. On the other hand, the integer arguments in the function are copies of the arguments in the calling function. Counting *start* up to the value of *j* does not change the value of *st* in the calling function.

Pointers to arrays. Since a string is an array, a pointer to a string is a special case of a pointer to an array. Just as an argument that's the name of a string is really a pointer, an argument that is the name of an array is also a pointer.

For example, you could have an array of the amounts of the checks you wrote last month, and a function that returns the subscript of the largest check. Declare the array like this:

```
float check[50];
```

Change the number within brackets if you write more checks or fewer checks. Write statements to store the amounts of your checks in the array, and assign the value of 50 to variable *n*. Then call function *big( )*:

```
s = big (check, n);
```

Function *big( )*:

```
big (num, size) /* Find largest number in array */
float num[ ];
int size;
{
float n = 0;
int i, j;
```

Chapter 6

```
for (i = 0; i < size; i = i + 1)
   if (num[i] > n) {
      n = num[i];
      j = i;
   }
return(j);
}
```

The declarator for formal argument *num* has no value within the brackets; that's a sure giveaway. The argument is a pointer, not an array. Since it is a pointer, the compiler doesn't care how many elements the array has. It reserves two bytes for one pointer, taking note that it is a pointer to type **float**. The amounts of the checks are accessed from the actual array in the calling function and compared to value *n*. The amount of the first check is certain to be greater than 0, the initial value of *n*. So the function sets *n* to the amount of the first check and *j* to 0, the subscript of the amount in *n*. If another check is larger than the first, its amount goes in *n* and its subscript goes in *j*. After looking at all check amounts, function *big()* returns the subscript of the largest amount, or the first of the largest amounts when there is a tie.

You could write the same function to use a pointer like this:

```
big (num, size) /* Find largest number in array */
float *num;
int size;
{
float n = 0;
int i, j;
for (i = 0; i < size; i = i + 1) {
   if (*num > n) {
      n = *num;
      j = i;
   }
   num = num + 1;
}
return(j);
}
```

The pointer to the formal argument *num* is the same whether *num* is an array or a single value. It contains the address of the argument, in this case, the first element of an array. In the **if** statement and the assignment statement that

Arrays and Pointers

follows, use the pointer instead of the array name and a subscript. Take a close look at the assignment statement that follows the **if**. It assigns *num + 1* to pointer *num*. This is intended to count the pointer up to element 1 of the array. The declarator for pointer *num* tells the compiler that *num* is a pointer to **float** type data. So when translating *num + 1*, the compiler adds 4, the number of bytes required for a type **float** number, to the pointer. The rest of the function is the same in both versions.

The second example uses *pointer arithmetic* to work its way through all the values in the array; it deserves a closer look. The integer following the plus sign is always multiplied by the length of an element to get the number of bytes that is added to the pointer. That is, the number is the number of elements, not the number of bytes. The operator does not have to be a plus sign, either. A minus sign works the same way. But what if the pointer is not a pointer to an array, but to a single element? Or what if adding to the pointer makes it point to an address beyond the end of the array? The address resulting from the expression you supply is used. It's your job to see that it is right. There is really no way the compiler can check on it, because the number of elements in the array is not always available to the compiler. The array may be declared in another file. As far as a function is concerned, it can be called by any other function.

Why bother with pointers, when the array notation does a good job? To give you an alternative way to write the function. It's really just a matter of semantics. The compiler does the same thing, whichever notation you use. Neither way is best in all cases.

In this example, the array notation used in the first version is best because the brackets in the declarator remind you that the argument is an array and the function returns a subscript, so subscript addressing results in a smaller function.

If the function returned a pointer, then pointer notation would be best because you would not have to declare and initialize an integer to use for the array subscript, and you would have the pointer value ready to return, without having to use the ampersand (**&**) operator.

Besides, you can do things with pointers that you cannot do otherwise. Learning to use them for arrays makes it easier to use them when you have to.

85

Chapter 6

An Array of Pointers

C allows you to have arrays of everything—even pointers. The most obvious need for an array of pointers is for sorting strings or structures. Although there are many ways to sort data, all of them at some point compare two data items and swap them if they are not in the desired order. Many swaps are performed in the course of sorting even just a few items. Swapping pointers instead of arrays or structures can save processing time.

When you sort data, you always have a *key* to sort by. For example, if you have a mailing list of names and addresses, you may want to sort it by zip codes. Then, when you print the mailing labels and put them on the envelopes, the mail is presorted by zip code, making the post office people happy. In that case, the zip code is the sort key. The key could be the name, address, or other information in the mailing list entry.

One sort method starts by comparing the keys in the first two structures, swapping them if they are not in the desired sequence. Then it compares the key in the second structure to that in the third structure. This continues until the keys in all structures have been compared. At the end of the first time through the data, the last structure is in its final sorted position. That is, if you are sorting in ascending sequence, the record having the greatest value for its key is the last structure. The process is repeated, resulting in two structures in correct sequence. Each time through the data, the number of structures compared is reduced by one. When the number of structures sorted is down to two, and they have been swapped if necessary, the sort is done. This is called a *bubble* sort because the structures rise, like bubbles, to the top of the array.

If you use an array of pointers that contain the addresses of the structures, the comparisons take a little longer because access using a pointer is indirect. But the swapping is much quicker. To rebuild the array in sorted order, access the structures in the order of the pointers in the pointer array.

Another technique to speed up this sort is to store the subscript of each pointer you swap in a variable. At the end of each pass through the array, all pointers that have subscripts for keys greater than the key in the stored subscript are in the proper sequence. Use the stored value as the limit of the next pass.

Arrays and Pointers

The declarator for the mailing list array is something like this:

```
#define SIZE
struct ml {
  char name[20];
  char addr[20];
  char city[12];
  char state[12];
  long int zip;
} mail[SIZE];
```

SIZE is a *symbolic constant* that represents the number of structures in array *mail*. Use a symbolic constant for an array size instead of a numeric constant. The symbol is more meaningful and the value can be more easily changed. Use a **#define** compiler control line as described in Chapter 10 to assign an appropriate value to *SIZE*.

Declare an array for the pointers like this:

```
struct ml *pmail[SIZE];
```

The symbolic constant enclosed in brackets tells the compiler that this is an array. The asterisk (*) ahead of the data name identifies an array of pointers. The keyword **struct** makes it an array of pointers to structures, and tag *ml* specifies that the structures are like those declared for array *mail*. But you must put the addresses of the structures in array *mail* into pointer array *pmail*. One way to initialize array *pmail* is:

```
for(i = 0; i < SIZE; i = i + 1)
  pmail[i] = &mail[i];
```

You have to put the names and addresses into array *mail* also; you can initialize the pointer at the same time. When both arrays have been initialized, you're ready to call the sorting function:

```
sort (pmail,SIZE);
```

Function *sort( )* is not as large as you might expect:

```
sort(parray,num) /* Sort mailing list by zip code */
struct ml *parray[ ];
int num;
{
struct ml *stor;
int limit, top, i;
```

Chapter 6

```
limit = num − 1;
while (limit > 1) {
  top = 0;
  for (i = 0; i < limit; i = i + 1)
    if ((*parray[i]).zip > (*parray[i+1]).zip) {
    stor = parray[i];
    parray[i] = parray[i + 1];
    parray[i + 1] = stor;
    top = i+1;
    }
  limit = top;
  }
return;
}
```

The executable statements of the function correspond to the sorting technique described earlier. Notice, though, the **if** statement in which the function accesses the zip code within each structure in the array. Since array *parray* is an array of structure pointers, *parray[i]* is a structure pointer and *(*parray[i])* is a structure. Because the program assigned the addresses of the structures in array *mail* to the pointers in array *pmail*, and because array *pmail* is the argument that is passed to *parray*, item *(*parray[i]).zip* in the **if** statement is member *zip* of structure *mail[i]*. The *membership operator,* a period (.), applies to a member of a structure even when the structure name is expressed with a pointer in a pointer array.

There's another operator that you can use with pointers to structures to access structure members. That operator is called the *indirect membership* operator. Like several other operators, it's the combination of two characters, the hyphen (–) and the greater than (>) symbol: ->. Here is the **if** statement of the sort function rewritten using the indirect membership operator:

```
if (parray[i]->zip > parray[i+1]->zip) {
  stor = parray[i];
  parray[i] = parray[i + 1];
  parray[i + 1] = stor;
  top = i;
  }
```

To avoid confusion between the period (.) and the indirect operator (->), remember the rules:

Arrays and Pointers

1. Use the membership operator with a structure name.
   Examples:

   mail[i].name

   (*parray[i]).name

2. Use the indirect membership operator with a pointer to a structure.
   Examples:

   parray[i]->name

   (&mail[i])->name

   Arrays and pointers give C a lot of power. The language provides several ways to use the capabilities of arrays and pointers. Learning to use them is not easy; it's probably the most difficult part of C for most people. But you can do it; it's not a problem, just a challenge.

Chapter 7
Expressions

Chapter 7
Expressions

Many expressions are similar in BASIC and C. Chapter 3 describes those expressions. But C has some additional *operators* that you can use in your expressions. Also, C has some different expressions that are handy. The new operators and the new expressions are the subject of this chapter.

Operators
The arithmetic operators are nearly the same in both languages. The one difference is that BASIC uses keyword MOD for the modulo division operator; C uses the percent sign (%). The relational operators are the same except for equal (==) and not equal (!=).

Equal relational operator. The equal relational operator (==) deserves special attention because you'll take your program apart character by character looking for the error when you use = instead of ==.

As a BASIC programmer, you're accustomed to using = in a relational expression. In BASIC, an equal sign in a relational expression is always a relational operator. In C, it is valid to have either an assignment equal or a relational equal in an expression, even where a relational expression would often be used. So the compiler does not consider the use of = instead of == an error, and your program compiles nicely. But it may not give you correct answers.

Here's an **if** statement that is quite acceptable to your C compiler:

if (a = b) /* Does not compare a to b! */

This statement assigns the value of variable *b* to variable *a*. If this value is equal to zero (false), the next statement is skipped. Otherwise the next statement is performed. Whether or not *a* and *b* are equal before this statement, they are equal afterward. But whatever processing is intended to be

93

Chapter 7

performed if they are equal is performed only if *b* is not equal to zero. Not quite what was intended.

The capability of having both = and == in an **if** statement is not all bad. This kind of statement is very handy:

if ((c = getchar( )) == EOF)

Function **getchar( )**, like most input functions, returns a character while the characters last, and EOF when the characters are all gone. The **if** statement is followed by a statement or block of statements to be performed when all the data has been read. Meanwhile, *c* contains the character that was read. By the way, *c* must be declared as an *integer* because EOF is an integer, not a character. Chapter 9 describes the I/O functions in detail. Also notice the parentheses around ((c = getchar( )). These are required because == has a higher priority than =, and without them, variable *c* is set to 0 (false) when a character is returned and to 1 (true) when EOF is returned.

Logical operators. The advent of computers in the military and in industry sparked an interest in Boolean algebra, which concerns the logical operations provided by BASIC and C. Boolean algebra actually doesn't relate to the *use* of computers as much as to their design. Still, the logical operations come in handy in some programs.

As an operand for a logical operation, an integer has a value of true or false. A zero value is taken as a false value. When a relational expression yields a true result, the result is 1. However, an integer is taken as a true value when its value is not equal to 0. C logical operators &&, ||, and ! apply to integers. These operators are similar to the AND, OR, and NOT operators of BASIC.

As an example of the use of logical operations, consider making a decision about taking a vacation. If you had a week off coming up and if you had more than $5,000, or if someone would give you money for it, you could go to Hawaii for a vacation. As a logical expression in BASIC, it looks like this:

300 HAWAII = DAYSOFF > 5 AND CASH > 5000 OR GIFT > 2000

The dollar amounts may vary, but if you have the time and money, this statement sets variable HAWAII to −1, BASIC's value for true. In C, the equivalent is:

hawaii = daysoff > 5 && cash > 5000 || gift > 2000;

Expressions

The C program does not always evaluate the complete expression. If *daysoff* > 5 is false, the value of *hawaii* is false (0), and the program does not evaluate the other two relational expressions. Similarly, if *daysoff* > 5 and *cash* > 5000 are both true, the value of *hawaii* is true (1). Only if *daysoff* > 5 is true and *cash* > 5000 is false does the program evaluate *gift* > 2000. You have to write logical expressions carefully; they don't always mean the same thing to the compiler as they do to you.

In the same BASIC program, you might have this statement:

350 IF NOT HAWAII THEN END

The expression NOT HAWAII would be true if HAWAII were false; you'll stay home. The C statement uses a different operator:

```
if (!hawaii)
    return;
```

BASIC provides additional logical operators: XOR, EQV, and IMP. You may need XOR (exclusive OR) now and then, but unless you are really into logical applications, you probably never use EQV or IMP. Before discussing these operations and how you can combine C operations to do the same thing, there's another type of logical operation to look at. Since a logical variable has only one of two values, it can be stored in a single bit. It doesn't need to use up a whole 16-bit integer. So why not perform the logical operation on each bit of the integer? C provides the *fields* structure to assign variable names to the bits of an unsigned integer; it also provides four bit-by-bit logical operations for you to use: inversion, and, or, and exclusive or.

Inversion changes every one (true) bit in the integer to a zero (false) bit, and every zero bit to a one bit. The operator is the tilde (~). Here's an example:

```
a = ~b;
```

Assuming that both *a* and *b* are unsigned integers, every bit in *a* is set to the value opposite that of the corresponding bit of *b*. That is, where *b* has a 1, *a* has a 0, and vice versa. It is like the ! operation, but it works on bits instead of integers.

The operator for the and operation is &. It is exactly like the && operation except that it performs the and operation on each of 16 bits of an unsigned integer at the same time. Here's an example:

```
if (a & b)
```

Chapter 7

This example assumes that *a* is an unsigned integer containing several flags, and that *b* is a mask, an unsigned integer with only one bit set. The bit of *b* that is set corresponds to a flag to be tested. The statement following the **if** statement is performed if the flag is set (true). That statement is skipped if the flag is not set (false). Similarly, the bit-by-bit or operation is identical to the || operation, but on each bit. The operator is |. Use this operation to set flags in an unsigned integer that contains flags:

a = a | b;

Assuming that *a* contains flags and that the only bits set to 1 in *b* are bits corresponding to flags that you want to set, this example statement sets those flags in *a*.

C has no exclusive or operation for logical variables, but it has a bit-by-bit exclusive or operation. An *exclusive or* operation on two logical variables yields a true result when either is true, but not both. The result is false if both variables have the same value, either true or false. For example, if you have an appointment with two people at the same time, and one shows up (is true), but the other one doesn't (is false), the result is good (true). If neither shows up (both are false), the result is that you have nothing to do at that time (false). But if both show up (both are true), you've got a problem (false result). The operator for the exclusive or operation is the ^. Here's an example:

if (!(a ^ b))

This example can test that two or more flags in *a* are set to a desired pattern of ones and zeros. The bits of *a* that are not being tested and the corresponding bits of *b* must be set to zero. The bits of *b* are set to the desired pattern. The exclusive or operation sets all bits of the result to zero except the bit(s) corresponding to flag(s) that are not set to the desired value(s). That is, the result is zero if the flags in *a* are set in the desired pattern. The not operator (!) sets the result true if the flags are correct, and the statement following the **if** is executed. Otherwise, that statement is skipped.

If you need an exclusive or operation between two logical variable integers, you can use the bit-by-bit operator. But you must make certain that the value of each logical variable integer is either zero or one. If any other nonzero value is used as

Expressions

a true value, the result is not valid. Here's an example:

c = a ^ b;

When either integer *a* or *b* has a value of one and the other has a value of zero, integer *c* is assigned the value of one (true). When integers *a* and *b* are either both zero or both one, integer *c* is set to zero (false).

The EQV (equivalence) operator of BASIC yields a true result when the two operands are true or when both are false. The result is false when the operands have opposite values. You can use a combination of C logical operators to get the equivalent result. Here's how:

if ((a || !b) && (!a || b))

The statement following the **if** statement is performed only when *a* and *b* are both true or are both false.

The *implication* operator of BASIC (IMP) deserves an explanation, even though it is seldom used. It is derived from the idea that the first operand implies the second. When the values of the operands are consistent with that relationship, the result of the implication operation is true. When the values of the operands violate the relationship, the result is false.

For example, working implies receiving wages. You could express this as a BASIC statement:

450 STATE = WORK IMP WAGES

There are four possible combinations of values of the two variables:

WORK	WAGES	WORK IMP WAGES
True	True	True
True	False	False
False	True	True
False	False	True

In the first case, the result is obviously true. In the second case, the worker was ripped off, the implication was violated, and the result is false. In the third case, the worker was lucky, but the result is true because the implication was not violated. In the fourth case, the implication holds and the result is true.

You can perform the implication operation using a combination of C logical operations:

state = !work || wage;

97

Chapter 7

The implication operation can be expressed as an or operation. The operands are the result of a not operation on *work* and *wage*. This statement assigns that result to *state*.

Logical operations are not widely used, but are needed now and then. C provides logical operations on integers considered as logical variables and on the corresponding bits of unsigned integers.

Shift operations. The shift operations are bit-by-bit operations on integers. BASIC does not provide shift operations. C provides a left-shift (<<) and a right-shift (>>) operation.

A left-shift operation shifts the bits in an integer by a specified number of bit positions. For example,

a = b << 3;

This statement says to shift the bits of integer *b* to the left by three bit positions and assign the result to *a*. The three leftmost bits are discarded. The three rightmost bit positions vacated by the shift are filled with zeros. This is a quick way to multiply the integer by 8. The multiplier in a left-shift operation is 2 to the power of the shift operand. In this case, the shift operand is 3; 2 to the third power is 8.

The right-shift operation shifts the bits in an integer to the right a specified number of bits. Here's an example:

a = b >> 3;

This statement says to shift the bits of integer *b* to the right by three bit positions and assign the result to integer *a*. The three rightmost bits are discarded. The three leftmost bit positions vacated by the shift are filled with zeros when integer *b* is unsigned. When integer *b* is signed (type **int**), the bit positions are filled with the leftmost bit of *b* before shifting (Lattice C for 8086/8088 microprocessors). The bit used to fill vacated bit positions on the left may be zero for all integers on some computers.

Shifting to the right three bit positions is a quick division by 8. Other shift values divide by other powers of 2, as in multiplying by shifting to the left. Shifts are also used to reformat the bits of an integer. The result of shifting by more than 15 or by a negative number is unpredictable.

sizeof operator. The **sizeof** operator is a very handy operator; it provides the size, in bytes, of a variable, array, or structure. Or it can provide the size of a data type. For example,

n = sizeof names;

Expressions

This statement causes the compiler to set variable *n* to the number of bytes reserved for array *names*. Notice that the value of operator **sizeof** and its operand is a constant, and that it is determined by the compiler at the time the program is compiled. The value is determined from the declarators.

For example, if you had declared a character array *names* with room for ten characters, the example would set *n* to 10, the size of the array. The length of string *names* would be the actual length of the *string*, zero until the program stored a string in the array. You need function **strlen( )** to give you the length of the string. Sometimes you need the length of a data type in your program. Use the **sizeof** operator like this:

s = sizeof (double);

This example sets variable *s* to eight.

Cast operator. Occasionally, it is necessary to force a variable to a type other than its declared type. The *cast* operator causes the program to convert the variable to the specified type in that expression only. The cast operator is a type keyword enclosed in parentheses. For example,

x = log ((double) y);

The **log( )** function in the Lattice C standard library requires a type **double** argument. The compiler doesn't know this and therefore cannot provide automatic type conversion. Therefore, assuming that *y* has been declared type **float** or **int**, the cast operator is needed to force *y* to type **double**.

Use the cast operator only when necessary. Forcing variables to different types indiscriminately can cause problems. A good rule for the cast operator is if in doubt, don't.

Increment and decrement operators. These two operators are shorthand for assignment statements; they can be used in expressions or as the only expressions in statements. You can use one in a **for** statement like this:

for (i = 0; i < 9; i++)

The expression **i++** means i = i + 1. It is probably the handiest operator in the entire C language. You can use it as the subscript of an array:

number[i++] = value[j++];

This statement means to copy *value[j]* into *number[i]*, to add 1 to the value of *j* after accessing *value[j]*, and to add 1 to

Chapter 7

the value of *i* after accessing *number[i]*. Here's another way to copy array elements:

`*pnumber++ = *pvalue++;`

This uses the ++ operator with pointers to copy array *value* into array *number*. Handy, isn't it? Here's another valid way to use this operator:

`i++;`

That is a statement all by itself; it means i = i + 1. All of these examples have shown the operator following its operand. This causes the addition to be done after the operand is used. It makes a difference in some cases, but not in all. Of these four examples, only the two examples that copy an array require the ++ to follow the operand. Placing the increment operator following the operand is called using it as a *postfix*.

You can also use the ++ operator as a *prefix*. Then the addition is performed first, before the operand is used. Here's an example:

```
main (argc,argv) /* Skip string 0 */
int argc;
char *argv[ ];
{
char in[15], out[15];
if (argc > 1)
   strcpy(in,*++argv);
else
   return;
if (argc > 2)
   strcpy(out,*++argv);
else
return;
}
```

This is an example of the first few lines of a program that reads one file and writes another file. It is convenient to type the file specifications following the program name when you run the program. Remember the example in Chapter 4, in which you type in a number after the program name? MS-DOS supplies any information you type after the program name in an array of strings, referred to in this example by its conventional name, *argv*. The number of strings is supplied as an integer, *argc*. The first string is always c. This program stores the second and third strings in arrays *in* and *out*, after checking the

Expressions

value of *argc* to be sure the strings were typed. It uses a pointer, which originally contains the address of string 0. The ++ operator ahead of the pointer skips string 0 and moves string 1 into array *in*. A similar statement stores string 2.

The increment operator is a very useful operator because you can use it either before or after the operand. But you must be careful to place the operator so that it performs the addition when it should be performed.

You don't always want to start at the beginning and move toward the end; sometimes you start at the end and work your way backward. C provides the −− operator, which subtracts 1 from the operand, for those occasions:

```
for (i = 1250; i >= 0; i−−)
  if (par[i] == '.')
    last = i;
```

This statement finds the last period in the text stored in array *par* and stores the subscript of that period in variable *last*. Like the increment operator, the decrement operator can be used with all kinds of variables, including pointers. It can be either a prefix or a postfix.

Handy as they are, there are places where you should not use the increment or the decrement operator:

1. Do not use these operators on a variable that is used elsewhere in the same expression.
2. Do not use these operators on a variable that is part of more than one argument of a function call.

The reason for these caveats is that you won't know where to put the operator to get the desired results. Often, you want to alter the value of the operand before or after any other operation is performed so that the same value of the variable applies in the entire expression or activation of the function. The order in which operations are performed and the order in which arguments are processed vary from compiler to compiler and from computer to computer. So even if (by good luck or after a few tries) you get it to work right, it may not work correctly when someone else uses it on another computer.

Operator Priority

Each operator of C, like each BASIC operator, has a priority that determines which of several operators in a statement is

Chapter 7

performed first. But because C has more operators, the priority list gets longer and more complicated. Table 7-1 lists the operators and their priorities, highest to lowest.

The priorities are similar to BASIC's for the operations that are common to both languages. In both languages, use parentheses (as in algebra) to force a different priority when necessary. A good rule is if in doubt, use parentheses.

The operators that have only one operand (unary operators) all have the second highest priority; they are on the second line of the table. Three of these use the same symbols as other operations having a lower priority. The minus sign (−) means either a unary minus (negative number) or subtraction. The asterisk (*) means either indirection or multiplication. The ampersand (&) means either the address of or a bit-by-bit logical AND operation. The way you use the operator in a statement (context) determines which operation you mean and which priority applies.

The column on the right in Table 7-1 shows the association of operands with operators. For example, the assignment operators (second lowest priority) assign the value of the portion to the right of the operator to the variable to the left of the operator. That is, they associate from right to left. In general, the association of operands with operators is the same as in BASIC.

Table 7-1. Operator Priority and Association

Operator(s)									Associates
( ) [ ] −> .									L–R
! ~ ++ −− − type) * & sizeof									R–L
* / %									L–R
+ −									L–R
<< >>									L–R
< <= > >=									L–R
== !=									L–R
&									L–R
^									L–R
|									L–R
&&									L–R
||									L–R
?: (conditional expression)									R–L
= += −= *= /= %= >>= <<= &= ^= |=									R–L
, (in **for** statement)									L–R

Expressions

Expressions
The additional expressions of C are more shorthand. They don't do anything that can't be done with expressions already described. But each is a more concise way of accomplishing the task. These additional expressions are the conditional expression and a whole family of assignment expressions.

Conditional expression. The *conditional expression* is a BASIC IF-THEN-ELSE all in one expression. In BASIC you might write:

740 IF A$ <= "Z" THEN A$ = A$ ELSE A$ = CHR$(ASC(A$) − 32)

If A$ is always a letter, uppercase or lowercase, this converts lowercase letters to uppercase without altering uppercase letters. A conditional expression is called for:

a[i] = (a[i] <= 'Z')? a[i]: a[i] − 0x20;

This conditional expression is used in an assignment statement. The conditional expression is the part of the statement to the right of the equal sign. The value of that expression is a[i] when a[i] is an uppercase letter. When a[i] is a lowercase letter, the value of the expression is a[i] − hexadecimal 20.

You can use a conditional expression anywhere you can use any other expression; here's one in a function call:

for (i = 0; i < 9; i++)
 printf ("%d%c",num[i],(i % 3 == 2)? '\n': ' ');

This statement displays three numbers from an integer array *num* on each of three lines. Don't let the percent signs inside the quotation marks get confused with the percent sign between *i* and 3. The percent signs within quotation marks have a special meaning for function **printf( )**, an output function described in Chapter 9. The characters enclosed in quotation marks are the *conversion specification*. This specification tells the **printf( )** function to display a decimal number followed by a character. The number is an element of array *num*. The character is the value of the conditional expression.

The percent sign between *i* and 3 is the modulo division operator. This modulo division operation divides *i* by 3 and provides the remainder (not the quotient) as the result. When the *num[0]* and *num[1]* are displayed, *i* % 3 is not equal to 2, and the value of the conditional expression is a space, which is displayed after each number. When *num[2]* is displayed, the

103

Chapter 7

relational portion of the conditional expression is true, and a new line character following the number starts a new line on the screen. The conditional expression works the same way for the other two lines of numbers.

The conditional expression is a concise way to program many conditional actions.

Assignment expressions. BASIC has an assignment statement using the = assignment operator. The C assignment statement is identical and uses the same operator. You can also use the assignment statement in an expression that is part of another statement. The section of this chapter on the equal relational operator (==) includes an example of an assignment expression. But C has more goodies. Look at this BASIC statement:

420 TOTAL = TOTAL + N

Translating this to C is nothing new. But there's a shortcut:

total += n;

The expression in this statement says to add the value of *n* to the value of *total* and assign the sum to *total*. It is exactly equivalent to:

total = total + n;

Besides being more concise, this *assignment operator* has some other advantages. Since the computer accesses the variable to the left of the equal sign only once, the program is usually more efficient. And you write the name of that variable only one time. With a simple name like *total*, that is no big deal. But with a name like *pmail[i]->name[j]*, it not only makes writing the statement easier, but it eliminates a possible source of error.

Most of the operators that require two operands can be used with the equal sign as an *assignment operator*. Here's the complete list:

+=   -=   *=   /=   %=   &= |=   ^=   <<=   >>=

Use these just as the example uses += to perform the indicated operation on two operands and assign the result to the first operand. The shift assignment operators are less obvious:

status >>= 3;

This shifts integer *status* three bits to the right, discarding the three rightmost bits and reformatting the *status* variable.

Expressions

An Example
In this chapter, the examples given with the descriptions of the operators and statements have shown a statement or two rather than a function or program. Here's a function that includes some of the new operators and expressions:

```
int deck[53] = {0, 0, 0, 0, 0, 0, 0, 0, 0, 0, 0, 0, 0,
                0, 0, 0, 0, 0, 0, 0, 0, 0, 0, 0, 0, 0,
                0, 0, 0, 0, 0, 0, 0, 0, 0, 0, 0, 0, 0,
                0, 0, 0, 0, 0, 0, 0, 0, 0, 0, 0, 0, 0, 1};
char *suit[ ] = {"Hearts","Diamonds","Spades","Clubs"};
char *card[ ] = {"Ace","2","3","4","5","6","7","8","9",
                 "10","Jack","Queen","King"};
draw( ) /* Draw a card */
{
int n;
n = 52;
while (deck[n] != 0) {
   n = rand( );
   n %= 52;
   }
deck[n] = 1;
printf ("Your card is %s of %s\n", card[n % 13],
       suit[n/13]);
return;
}
```

The arrays are declared before the function for two reasons:

1. To be able to initialize the values.
2. To make the arrays accessible to other functions that might need to access them.

Array *deck* contains a flag integer for each card in the deck and an extra flag to get started with. You can set flags 0–51 to 0, but leave *deck[52]* set to 1. Arrays *suit* and *card* contain the names of the cards.

The function contains a **while** loop that insures that a card is drawn only once. Setting *n* to 52 insures that the statements in the loop are executed at least once. The first statement calls function **rand( )** to obtain a positive random integer, which it assigns to *n*. The next statement sets *n* to the remainder from dividing *n* by 52. The value of *n* represents a card that may already have been drawn. If so, the flag for that card

Chapter 7

is not equal to zero, and the loop is executed again. Otherwise, the card is valid.

The function next sets the flag corresponding to the drawn card and prints the name of the card, using the name arrays. Notice the expressions used as subscripts. The suit is the quotient and the card the remainder resulting from dividing *n* by 13.

Function **rand( )** is a random integer function supplied with the Lattice C standard library. It returns positive integers. You can use function **srand(seed)** in the calling function to re-seed the random number generator. Argument **seed** is an unsigned integer. Reseeding the generator and clearing the flag array (except for flag 52) shuffles the deck and starts a fresh hand. If you don't call function **srand( )**, or if you call it using a constant value as the seed, the sequence of cards is always the same. One way to get a random seed is to count in a loop that awaits input from the keyboard. The count is proportional to your reaction time. Chapter 8 gives an example of generating a random seed.

Now that you know about the shorthand expressions, you can write programs that *look* like C programs.

Chapter 8
Transferring Control

Chapter 8
Transferring Control

In Chapter 3, we discussed statements which operate in a similar manner in both C and BASIC, specifically **if**, **for**, and **goto**. In this chapter, we'll discuss other features of the **if** and **for** statements that make them more useful than those of BASIC. Also, this chapter will introduce the **do while**, **switch**, **break**, and **continue** statements that give C additional power.

The GOTO statement of BASIC can make it difficult to understand what a program is doing. Often, several GOTO statements transfer control to the same place so that the actual relationships between the parts of the program are not clear. But the control statements of BASIC are limited and the GOTO statement is needed. C's additional control statements clearly show the relationships and provide ways of expressing the same transfers. The idea is to have a control statement do the job without a **goto** so that the relationship between alternate parts of the program is clear.

else if Statement

Before you jump on me with both feet and tell me that BASIC also has ELSE IF capabilities, let me hasten to concede the point. But because the IF statement and all ELSE IFs must be included within the maximum length of a BASIC statement (255 characters), its use is limited. The C statement begins with a keyword or the name of a variable, array, structure, or function, and extends to a semicolon, with no maximum length. You can spread it over as many lines of the program as you like. This makes the **else if** statement quite different from a BASIC ELSE IF.

Here's a three-way branch:

```
if (age <= 12) {
   price = 1.00;
   child++;
   }
```

Chapter 8

```
else if (age <= 65) {
    price = 3.50;
    adult++;
    }
  else {
    price = 1.25;
    senior++;
}
```

This statement maintains totals for three groups, each of which pays a different price. When *age* is 12 or less, the price is $1.00, and 1 is added to total *child*. The remaining portions of this statement are skipped. When *age* is greater than 12 and less than or equal to 65, the price is $3.50, and 1 is added to total *adult*. When *age* is greater than 65, the price is $1.25, and total *senior* is increased by 1. The relationship between the parts of the statement that apply to the groups is clear. Variable *age* is not compared unnecessarily.

An **if** statement can have as many **else if**s as you like, but three or four is about all you really want. After that, it becomes difficult to understand what the statement means. The **switch** statement, described below, is appropriate when you need more choices.

for Loop

The examples of **for** loops from Chapter 3 up to this point are all very similar to those of BASIC. But semicolons divide the **for** statement into three parts:

1. Initialization
2. Test
3. Step

These parts correspond approximately to the *initial value*, *final value*, and *step value* in a FOR statement. But there, the similarity ends. In C, the parts do not have to be closely related; one part can be indirectly related to the others. Any part can be omitted. And the initialization and step parts can consist of one or more expressions.

The initialization expression (or expressions separated by commas) is performed first. Then the test expression is evaluated. If it's false (value equal to zero), the rest of the statement is skipped. If it's true (value not equal to zero), the statement or block of statements that follow the **for** statement is executed. Then the step expression (or expressions) is executed,

Transferring Control

and the test expression is evaluated again. First, here's an example of a **for** statement having more than one initialization statement:

```
for (i = 0,j = strlen(master);j >= 0;i++)
   retsam[i] = master[--j];
retsam[++i] = '\0';
```

Arrays *retsam* (master spelled backward) and *master* are strings; *i* and *j* are integers. The statement copies the characters of *master* into *retsam* in reverse order until the entire string has been copied. The statement on the last line of the example puts a null character at the end of array *retsam*, making it a valid string.

Here's an example of a **for** statement with no initialization expression and two step expressions:

```
for (;old[j] != ' ';i++,j++)
   new[i] = old[j];
new[i] = '\0';
```

This statement copies a word from string *old* to string *new*. Other parts of the program have set *i* at the start of the desired word of *old*, so *i* doesn't need to be initialized. Index *j* is set to place the word in the proper place in string *new*; *j* doesn't need to be initialized, either. The statement moves the characters of the selected word. The step expressions update both *i* and *j*. When the next character of string *old* is a space, *i* points to the position of the character after the word in string *new*, and the loop terminates. The statement following the **for** statement places a null character after the word that was moved, completing the string. Notice that when you omit a portion of the **for** statement, you leave the semicolon(s) that separate the parts.

Even the test portion can be omitted, but the statements of the loop must contain some control statement to exit the loop. (Of course, you can always turn off your computer to stop.) Usually, it is best to put the exit condition in the test portion of the **for** statement. It is more obvious there, and you don't gain anything by putting it in the loop. But here's an example of an unusual **for** statement:

```
for (i = 0;!kbhit();i++)
   ;
```

Function *kbhit()* returns a false value when no key on the

111

Chapter 8

keyboard has been pressed since the last keyboard read function. When a character is waiting to be read, the function returns a true value. So, assuming no character is waiting to be read when the **for** statement is performed, the computer remains in this loop waiting for you to press a key.

Index variable *i* counts the number of times through the loop. The loop itself consists of a *null statement*. The semicolon is required; without it, the next statement would be executed as the loop statement. But all the computing is done in the **for** statement, so there is nothing to do in the loop.

If you use the loop to test reaction time, the initialization expression is necessary. But this statement is a good way to get a random value to use as a seed for the random number generator. In that case, you could use this:

```
for (;!kbhit();i++)
   ;
```

Variable *i* could have any value to start with, although it might tend to have the same value each time you run the program. Thus, it would not be a random value. But in any case, the result would be useful as a seed value.

When you press a key on the keyboard, the corresponding character is stored in a *queue* until a read function returns the character to a calling function. The number of characters that can be stored in the queue varies from one computer to the next. Function *kbhit()* continues to return a true value from the time a key is pressed until all characters in the queue have been read. If you do not read the characters, clear the queue before using function *kbhit()* again:

```
while (kbhit())
   getch();
```

The **for** loop can do the same things as the FOR-NEXT loop of BASIC, but the two are really not much alike. C gives you a whole new set of possibilities.

do while Loop

The **do while** loop is performed at least once. That is, the condition for repeating the loop is not tested until after the statement(s) of the loop have been executed.

You could get along without this type of loop, but there are applications that are simpler when you don't test the condition until the loop has been performed one time. If you use

Transferring Control

a **for** or **while** loop for those applications, you must fool the computer with the first result so that it performs the loop the first time.

The **draw( )** function in Chapter 7 is a case in point. Remember, it has an extra element set to 1 in array *deck* and an initialization statement to force a test of that element. Here's a revised version that uses a **do while** loop:

```
int deck[52] = {0, 0, 0, 0, 0, 0, 0, 0, 0, 0, 0, 0, 0,
                0, 0, 0, 0, 0, 0, 0, 0, 0, 0, 0, 0, 0,
                0, 0, 0, 0, 0, 0, 0, 0, 0, 0, 0, 0, 0,
                0, 0, 0, 0, 0, 0, 0, 0, 0, 0, 0, 0, 0};
char *suit[ ] =  {"Hearts","Diamonds","Spades","Clubs"};
char *card[ ] =  {"Ace","2","3","4","5","6","7","8","9",
                "10","Jack","Queen","King"};
draw( ) /* Draw a card—revised */
{
int n;

do {
  n = rand( );
  n %= 52;
  } while (deck[n] != 0);
deck[n] = 1;
printf ("Your card is %s of %s\n", card[n % 13],
  suit[n/13]);
return;
}
```

The statements of the loop obtain a value for variable *n* before the **while** statement tests the contents of *deck[n]*. If the array element contains 0, the loop is not repeated. If the element has already been set to 1, the loop is repeated until an unused number turns up. The **do while** loop improves this function significantly. It eliminates the extra element in array *deck*, one assignment statement *(n = 52)*, and one test of the value of *deck[n]* in each call of the function.

Whenever your program will be simpler if you can go through the loop one time before testing the repeat condition, try a **do while** loop instead of a **for** or **while**.

switch Statement

You can use a **switch** statement to good advantage in a program that has several options displayed on a menu. The user

113

Chapter 8

types a letter to select an option. Assuming the letter typed is in variable *sel*, here's the statement:

```
switch (sel) {
  case 'C' :
  case 'c' :
    copy(in_file,out_file);
    return;
  case 'E' :
  case 'e' :
    edit(in_file,out_file);
    return;
  case 'N' :
  case 'n' :
    new(out_file);
    return;
  case 'T' :
  case 't' :
    trans(in_file,out_file);
    return;
  default :
    printf("Invalid selection. Try again.");
}
```

In this case, the program has four options, each performed in a function. The statement compares the character in variable *sel* to the constant in the first **case** statement. When the characters do not match, the statement skips to the next **case** statement and compares the character to the constant in that statement. When the characters match, the statement performs the statements that follow the **case** statement. For example, if *sel* contains 'c', the statement calls function **copy( )**. A **return** statement following the function call returns control to MS-DOS—assuming this statement is in function *main( )*.

To allow either an uppercase or lowercase letter to select the proper function, there are two **case** statements preceding each function call. If, for example, *sel* contains 'C', the **case** statement for 'c' is ignored, and function **copy( )** is called. The rule is that after the **switch** statement finds a matching **case**, the following **case** statements are ignored and all other following statements are performed. A **return** statement or a **break** statement (described in the next section) is required to get out of the **switch** statement.

Transferring Control

When *sel* doesn't match the constant in any **case** statement, the statement following the **default** statement is performed. In this example, it is a print function that displays a message. The **switch** statement doesn't automatically repeat itself; your program has to call an input function to get another selecting character and perform the **switch** statement again. You don't have to put a **default** statement in your **switch** statement. If you choose not to, the statement that follows the **switch** statement is performed when no match occurs.

The **switch** statement has several limitations.

1. The parentheses that follow keyword **switch** must enclose a variable name or an expression. The variable must be either an integer or character; the expression must evaluate to an integer or a character. Neither a string nor a real number is allowed.
2. Keyword **case** must be followed by a constant or an expression that consists of constants.
3. No two **case** statements can have the same constant value.

Here's another example that shows what happens when you do not include a **break** or **return** statement:

```
switch (n) {
  case 5:
    printf("Please, ");
  case 4:
    printf("Mr. ");
  case 3:
    printf("Smith, ");
  case 2:
    printf("%con't ",(n == 2)? 'D': 'd');
  case 1:
    printf("%co!\n",(n == 1)? 'G': 'g');
}
```

If *n* is 5, all the **printf( )** function calls are performed, and the result on your screen is:

Please, Mr. Smith, don't go!

You get a curt message when *n* is 3:

Smith, don't go!

If that doesn't have the desired effect, don't lose your cool. Just make *n* equal to 1:

Go!

115

Chapter 8

Changes the meaning a little, doesn't it? The point is that all the statements starting with the selected statement are executed.

The **switch** statement, even with its limitations, is a valuable addition to your programming repertoire.

break Statement

The **break** statement gets you out of the block of statements in a **for**, **while**, **do while**, or **switch** statement. Take another look at the first example of a **switch** statement, with the **returns** replaced with **breaks**:

```
switch (sel) {
  case 'C' :
  case 'c' :
    copy(in_file,out_file);
    break;
  case 'E' :
  case 'e' :
    edit(in_file,out_file);
    break;
  case 'N' :
  case 'n' :
    new(out_file);
    break;
  case 'T' :
  case 't' :
    trans(in_file,out_file);
    break;
  default :
    printf("Invalid selection. Try again.");
}
```

In the first version, the **return** statement ended the program after a selected function had completed. In this version, the statement following the **switch** statement is executed when the selected function completes. By placing the **switch** statement in an appropriate loop, you can allow the user to perform more than one program option without having to start the program again.

Another good use for the **break** statement is in a search of a character array for a particular character. Here's an example:

Transferring Control

```
for(i = 0;text[i] != '?';i++)
  if (i == 20) {
    i = -1;
    break;
  }
```

This loop has two exit conditions: at the first question mark or at the end of the array. Notice that when the loop terminates, *i* contains the subscript of the first question mark, or −1 if the array doesn't contain a question mark. You could search for any of several characters in the string; the loop can have as many **break** statements as you need.

Break is a handy way to get out of a block of statements.

continue Statement

Sometimes you don't want to get out of a loop, but you're through processing a particular array member. The **continue** statement can be used in any loop to skip the rest of the statements in the block and continue processing the loop. For a **for** or **while** loop, this means going to the **for** or **while** statement at the beginning of the loop; for a **do while** loop, this means going to the **while** statement at the end of the loop. Here's an example:

```
fl = 1;
i = 0;
j = 0;
while (in[i] != '\0') {
  if(in[i] == ' ' && fl == 1) {
    i++;
    continue;
  }
  if(in[i] == ' ')
    fl = 1;
  else
    fl = 0;
  comp[j++] = in[i++];
}
```

This loop compresses a string by making a copy with no leading spaces and only one space between words. String *in* is to be compressed; string *comp* is the compressed copy. Variables *fl*, *i*, and *j* are integers. Flag *fl* is set to 1, and indexes *i* and *j* are set to 0. If string *in* has leading spaces, index *i* is increased by 1, and the **continue** statement skips the rest of the

Chapter 8

statements in the block. The first character that is not a space sets flag *fl* to 0 and is copied into string *comp*.

The next space sets flag *fl* to 1 before being copied into string *comp*. If the character after the space is another space, it's skipped. If the character after the space is not a space, flag *fl* is set to 0, and all characters are copied up to the next space.

The **continue** statement doesn't apply to the block of statements that follow a **switch** statement. If you place a **continue** statement in a **switch**, the **continue** statement continues a loop that includes the **switch**. If the **switch** is not part of a loop, the compiler issues an error message. The **continue** statement should be used with care, but it's ready to use when you need it.

An Example

When you have a table or a file of names, it's often helpful to find a particular name without comparing the desired name to every name in the table. Sorting the table makes finding the name easier, but it's not easy to add names to a sorted table. One technique used to solve this problem is hash coding.

A *hash code* is a numeric value derived from the name. An arbitrary number of hash codes are selected, and a table entry is reserved for each code. When you add a name to the table, you compute a hash code from the name and store the name in the corresponding entry. When you look for a name in the table, you compute the hash code and look in the corresponding entry for the desired name. Of course, the number of hash codes is usually not as great as the number of names that might have to be stored; there often is more than one name for each code. There are several good ways to solve this problem, but discussions of these ways do not belong in this book.

The function example for this chapter computes the hash code for a name passed to the function as an argument. The function uses a simple method of deriving a hash code. The number of hash codes is supplied in a **#define** compiler control line (see Chapter 10). Here's the function:

```
#define NUM 50
hash(name) /* Compute hash code */
char name[ ];
{
int letter, code = 0, i = 0;
```

Transferring Control

```
while (name[i] != '\0') {
  if (name[i] >= 'A' && name[i] <= 'Z')
    letter = name[i] - 0x40;
  else if (name[i] >= 'a' && name[i] <= 'z')
    letter = name[i] - 0x46;
    else if (name[i] == ' ' || name [i] == '.')
    letter = 0;
      else
        printf("Letters, spaces, and periods only!");
  code += letter;
  i++;
  }
return(code % NUM);
}
```

The function subtracts hexadecimal 40 from the ASCII code for an uppercase letter and hexadecimal 46 from the ASCII code for a lowercase letter. This provides a unique value from 1 through 52 for each letter of the alphabet. The function supplies zeros for spaces and periods, and displays an error message when any other character is supplied in the name. The value for each letter is added to variable *code*. The remainder that results from dividing the total by the number of hash codes is the hash code for argument *name*.

This function contains an example of a four-way switch using an **if else if** statement described in this chapter. A **switch** statement to do the job would have required 54 **case** statements.

Notice that the examples in this chapter take full advantage of C's ability to be concise. To really learn to use the features that streamline a C program, go back over the examples in earlier chapters and rewrite them using the increment and decrement operators, the conditional expression, and the assignment operators. Make them look like C programs.

All features and statements of C have now been described. Appendix A is a summary of the language for ready reference. The rest of the book describes the standard I/O functions, the compiler control directives, and compiling and debugging. While not part of the language, these things are very important. Don't stop now.

Chapter 9
Input/Output

Chapter 9
Input/Output

Input/output consists of the transfer of data between the microprocessor and various devices. These devices may be inside the computer, like disk drives, or peripheral devices connected by cables, like the monitor, keyboard, printer, and modem. Transferring data to and from these devices is an important part of the work your computer does.

Most other computer languages, including BASIC, have statements to perform input/output (I/O). C is unique; it has no I/O statements. Instead, it uses I/O functions. Like the functions you can write (described in Chapter 4), these functions have names and many of them have arguments. Each transfers data from a device (input) or to a device (output). The function name indicates the operation to perform and sometimes implies which device to use. The arguments supply additional information, for example, which device or file to use, where in memory to get or put the data, and how many characters to move. You can use the standard I/O functions much like you would use I/O statements. They're functions, not C statements.

Because C uses I/O functions, it's more *transportable* than most languages. That is, a program written for one computer can be used on another with few changes. Most of the problems of moving a program to another computer result from differences in I/O devices. When your program calls a standard I/O function, and the computer you move to has a version of that function which uses the same name and arguments, the program runs correctly on the new computer. Unless, of course, the version of the standard I/O function on the new computer doesn't do what it should. The transportability problem is one of selecting arguments that work on most computers and providing versions of the I/O functions that work on specific computers. The fact that the functions may not be exactly the same is unimportant—what is important is that they *perform* the same operations.

Chapter 9

This chapter first describes I/O for the keyboard and screen, with BASIC examples and the C equivalents. Then it describes I/O functions that don't correspond to BASIC statements. Finally, it describes file I/O and output to a printer.

Displaying Data

To display a message on the screen in BASIC, you use a PRINT statement, like this:

100 PRINT "The House of Seven Gables"

The **printf( )** function in the standard library supplied with your C compiler can display a string:

printf("The House of Seven Gables\n");

This is a special case of a call to the **printf( )** function. It has only one argument: the string to be displayed. The function name implies that the device is the *standard output device* defined by MS-DOS. Usually, this device is the screen, but with MS-DOS 2.0 (and newer versions) you can use redirection. *Redirection* occurs when you use the greater than (>) symbol and the name of a device or file to tell MS-DOS to direct output to another device or a file. See your MS-DOS manual for more information about redirection.

The first argument of **printf( )** is always a string, called the *control string*. In this special case, all the characters in the string are displayed. The last character, \n, is the *newline* character. When you use MS-DOS, the newline character is actually two characters: carriage return and linefeed. Function **printf( )** automatically supplies two characters when you give it a newline character to send to the screen. In BASIC, a PRINT statement always ends with a carriage return and linefeed unless you tell it otherwise with a semicolon or comma. In C, you use a newline character each time you go to a new line. You can have several in a control string, if necessary.

A control string usually contains one or more conversion specifications. Here's another BASIC example:

250 A$ = "cats and"
260 PRINT A%; A$; B%; "dogs make a lot of pets!"

Variables A% and B% contain numbers of cats and dogs. If A is 3 and B is 4, the statement displays:

3 cats and 4 dogs make a lot of pets!

The C equivalent requires declarators and a function call:

Input/Output

```
int a, b;
static char as[] = "cats and";
printf("%d %s %d dogs make a lot of pets!\n",a,as,b);
```

The first thing to notice about this function call is that it has four arguments. The **printf( )** function is an exception to the general rule that a C function has a fixed number of arguments. The **printf( )** function has a control string argument plus one argument for each conversion specification in the control string. This example control string contains three % characters, each of which begins a conversion specification; thus, the total number of arguments is four.

The first conversion specification, **%d**, is used with the first argument that follows the control string, variable *a*. Variable *a* is an integer; the conversion specification says to convert the integer into the ASCII representation of the decimal equivalent of the twos-complement integer. The next conversion specification, **%s**, displays a string. It applies to the next argument, variable *as*. No conversion is necessary; the string variable is displayed next. The third specification, **%d**, converts and displays variable *b*.

The positions of the conversion specifications in the control string determine where the variables are displayed. Variable *a* is first, then variable *as*, and last, variable *b*. Every character of a control string that is not part of a conversion specification is displayed in its relative position. That is, the spaces that separate the specifications appear between the variables in the display. The text that follows the third specification completes the line on the screen.

Table 9-1 lists the conversion specifications that you can use with the **printf( )** function.

Table 9-1. Conversion Specifications

Specification	Type of Conversion
%d	Decimal
%o	Octal
%x	Hexadecimal
%u	Unsigned integer
%f	Floating point
%e	Exponential format
%g	Either %e or %f
%s	Character string
%c	Single character

Chapter 9

The type of a variable determines which conversion specification to use. For type **int** or **short**, use **%d**, **%o**, or **%x**. The octal conversion doesn't apply to microcomputers because no utilities for microcomputers use octal numbers. Octal representation of a number uses digits 0–7. Use octal only if your program also runs on a computer that uses octal representation. Hexadecimal numbers are described in Appendix B. For type **long**, use an *l* ahead of the letter for any specification that applies to an integer; that is, use **%ld**, **%lo**, or **%lx**. For type **unsigned** use specification **%u**.

A floating-point number can be displayed with either **%f**, **%e**, or **%g**. The **%f** specification displays the value as a decimal number with a decimal point. You can place an .n modifier in front of the letter or letters to display only *n* digits to the right of the decimal point. For example, you should display dollar amounts with specification **%.2f** to show dollars and cents only.

The **%e** specification displays the value in exponential form; that is, a decimal number between 1 and 9.999999, an E, and a number that specifies a power of ten. You can use the .n modifier to limit the number of digits to the right of the decimal point. The **%g** specification uses either **%f** or **%g**, whichever is shorter. For type **double**, use an *l* just ahead of the letter; that is, use **%lf**, **%le**, or **%lg**.

For type **char**, use **%c** for single characters or **%s** for character strings. The .n modifier applies to specification **%s**, but with a different meaning. For a string, *n* is the maximum number of characters to display. For example, specification **%.10s** displays all of string "Hello!" but only ten characters of "Happy Birthday".

One modifier applies to all specifications: a number that specifies a minimum number of characters for the display of a variable. Place this number immediately following the percent sign (%).

Use this modifier to format the data in your display. For example, if the specification is **%20.2f**, and the value of the variable is 5.34, 16 spaces are inserted ahead of the 5. Using a loop to compute the variable and display it, this specification gives you a column of figures with the decimal points neatly aligned vertically.

By putting a minus sign (−) ahead of the value, the variable comes first, and additional spaces follow the characters of

Input/Output

the variable. The specification **%-10c** displays a character followed by nine spaces.

Using conversion specifications in the control string is similar to using formatting characters with a PRINT USING statement of BASIC:

400 PRINT USING "& $####.##";DAY$; AMT

Using the **printf( )** function:

printf("%s $%7.2f\n",day,amt);

This statement displays a line on the screen with the day followed by an amount:

Monday $ 75.82

More Display Functions

Do you ever use this statement in BASIC?

480 PRINT

It leaves a blank line in a display by sending a carriage return and linefeed to the screen. In C, the function to use is **putch( )**:

putch('\n');

You can use the **putch( )** function for any character, either a constant or a variable.

The **printf( )** function is ideal for displaying formatted data. When you have only a string to display, you can use the **puts( )** function:

puts("From BASIC to C");

This function displays the argument (a string constant in this case) followed by a newline character. The argument can be a string variable:

static char sub[ ] = "A new approach to C language";
puts(sub);

Getting Data from the Keyboard

The **scanf( )** function accepts characters from the keyboard, performs the specified conversions, and stores the results in the listed variables. In BASIC, you use the INPUT statement:

300 INPUT NAM$,AMT

The **scanf( )** function to read a string and a decimal value is:

scanf("%s%f",nam,&amt);

Chapter 9

The **scanf( )** function transfers data from the *standard input device* defined by MS-DOS. The standard input device is usually the keyboard, but users of MS-DOS 2.0 (and newer versions) can use redirection. The redirection character is the less than character (<); you can redirect input from a file or another input device. See your MS-DOS manual for more information about redirection.

The first argument for the **scanf( )** function is a control string similar to the control string for the **printf( )** function. The control string usually contains conversion specifications similar to those listed in Table 9-1. In the example, the control string specifies a string and a type **float** variable.

There are just a few differences in the conversion specifications for **scanf( )**. The **%g** specification doesn't apply to **scanf( )**, and the **%e** specification and **%f** specification both accept a real number without an exponent. The .n modifier doesn't apply to **scanf( )**. The optional number following the percent sign (field length modifier) is the maximum number of characters in the field.

The **scanf( )** function recognizes an additional conversion specification for type **short** variables: **%h**. You will probably not use it, because in Lattice C for MS-DOS, types **short** and **int** are the same size. The specification is a good thing to have, though, in case you want to compile a program written for another computer in which type **short** is different from type **int**.

Pay particular attention to the variable name arguments of the example statement. These arguments must be pointers. Since the name of a string or other array is a pointer, no **&** is needed with variable *nam*. But the name of any other type of variable must be preceded by an **&**. The Lattice C Compiler does not check that the arguments in function calls are the correct type. You will not get an error message when you leave out the **&**. Only when you run the program and get invalid results will you know something is wrong. This error can be very subtle.

When reading characters from the keyboard, **scanf( )** ignores spaces, tab characters, and newline characters (called white space) preceding other characters. A variable terminates at the first white space character.

Input/Output

This example of a BASIC INPUT statement is more typical:

450 INPUT "Number of meters: ", M%

You need two function calls for the C equivalent:

```
printf("Number of meters: ");
scanf("%d",&m);
```

That's not very streamlined, is it? Oh, well, you can't win them all. Anyhow, the two function calls are not very big.

More Input Functions

The standard I/O library includes an alternative to function **scanf( )** for reading strings. Here's an example:

```
gets(nam);
```

The **gets( )** function (get string) accepts characters from the keyboard until you press RETURN (the newline character). It stores these characters in string *nam*, substituting a null character for the newline character. The **gets( )** function is a handy substitute for **scanf( )** when you are reading a string that ends with a newline character.

You can read a single character with function **getche( )**:

```
key = getche();
```

Function **getche( )** (get character-echo) reads a character from the keyboard, displays it on the screen, and returns the character to the calling function. Variable *key* is set to the value of the character. Sometimes it's better to read data character by character instead of by strings.

If something you're typing in is so secret you don't even want to see it yourself, you can type a character without displaying it on the screen:

```
key = getch();
```

Function **getch( )** is similar to function **getche( )** except that it doesn't display the character. This function is useful when you're programming games or security functions. You often do not want to display the input to a game; passwords should never be displayed.

Using both **scanf( )** and **gets( )** functions in a program loop can cause a problem. Remember, any white space character completes the last variable of a call to **scanf( )**. The white space character is not discarded; it remains in the buffer.

Chapter 9

awaiting the next input operation from the keyboard. When the next operation is another **scanf( )** function, it ignores the white space character. But when the next input operation is a **gets( )** function, and the character loafing around in the buffer is a newline, the **gets( )** function returns a null string.

You don't have to change the **gets( )** function to correct the problem; there's a better solution:

```
while (getchar( ) != '\n')
    ;
```

This loop clears the newline character in the buffer. It calls the **getchar( )** function, which is similar to the **getche( )** function previously discussed, except that it gets a character from the buffer that **scanf( )** uses. Since all the processing is done in the **while** statement, the loop consists of a null statement. Place the loop after the call to the **scanf( )** function.

Sequential File Operations

When your program has files to read or write, it needs this statement ahead of any file operation:

```
#include <stdio.h>
```

This is a compiler control line that is usually the first statement in a program. Don't forget, the number sign (**#**) must be in column 1. It reads a file named **stdio.h** and makes it part of your program. File **stdio.h** comes with your compiler. It must be on the disk in the default drive at the time you compile the program. It contains compiler control lines and data declarations that your program needs to perform I/O operations. The next chapter fully describes compiler control lines.

Opening a file. Like a BASIC program, a C program must open a file before reading or writing data to the file. Opening a file consists of associating an identifier used in the program with the MS-DOS file specification. The BASIC example is:

100 OPEN "I", #1, "B:FILE1.DAT"

The "I" means that the file is an input file; #1 is the file number that you use in every statement of your program that refers to the file; and "B:FILE1.DAT" is the MS-DOS file specification.

In a C program, you must declare a file identifier for each file that is in use at the same time. The declarator is:

```
FILE *f1;
```

Input/Output

Once the declarator has been supplied, you can call function *fopen( )* anywhere in your program (within the scope of the declarator):

```
if ((f1 = fopen("B:FILE1.DAT","rb")) == NULL)
    printf("Can't open input file");
```

The function call begins with the file identifier *f1*, which is set to the pointer to the file if it is opened successfully or to NULL if an error occurs. The arguments are the file specification and a mode string that determines what you can do with the file. The mode string in the example is **rb** (for read).

You could put the function call in a separate statement, but you need the **if** statement either way; combining the two is more concise. If you tried to continue with *f1* equal to NULL instead of the file pointer, the first file operation would fail, and you might not be able to tell readily what had failed.

The other valid mode strings are:

wb   write
ab   append

A write file is one to which you can write, starting at the beginning of the file; an append file is one to which you can write, starting at the previous end of the file. Use **wb** when the file does not exist, or when you want to write over an existing file with the same file specification. Use **ab** to add to an existing file.

The letter *b* included in the mode strings is optional, but you need it to read and write file records similar to the examples in this section. Without the *b* (for binary) in the mode strings, the file is opened in the *translated* mode, and the I/O functions add a carriage return after each newline character. The internal representation of a number can have the same bit sequence as a newline character; if it does, the record is written incorrectly. To avoid this error, use the *b* when your file records contain internal representations of numbers (as the example record in this section does). When the records of your files consist entirely of text, omit the *b*.

Reading a record. To read a record from a sequential file in BASIC, you use an INPUT # statement, like this:

200 INPUT #1, TITLE$, PRICE

This statement reads a record from file #1 and assigns the string to variable TITLE$ and the real number to variable PRICE.

131

Chapter 9

The C equivalent requires a structure to define the record:

```
struct {
  char title[25];
  float price;
} seqrec;
```

The structure is ideal for this purpose because it can be specified to the file I/O functions by the structure name, yet each item in the record is accessible by its own name. For example, the title is *seqrec.title* and the price is *seqrec.price*.

The equivalent of the BASIC INPUT statement is a call to function **fread( )**:

if((x = fread(&seqrec,sizeof seqrec,1,fl)) == 1)

The **if** statement is followed by a block of statements that perform the desired processing of the record from the file. The **fread( )** function has four arguments. The first argument is the address of the structure, and the second is the size of the structure. Use the **sizeof** operator to obtain the size. The next argument, 1, is the number of records to write, and the fourth is the file identifier. The function returns the number of records it has read; a value less than that of the third argument indicates either an error or end-of-file. Use function **feof( )** to detect end-of-file.

Writing a record. To write a record to the file, assuming the file has been opened for writing, the BASIC statement is:

400 PRINT #1, TITLE$;",";PRICE

This statement writes a record to file #1, consisting of string TITLE$, a comma, and real number PRICE.

The equivalent C statement is:

if ((x = fwrite(&seqrec,sizeof seqrec,1,fl)) != 1)

The **if** statement should be followed by a statement or block of statements to be performed in the event of an error. Function **fwrite( )** is very similar to function **fread( )**. The arguments are identical, but the function writes a record instead of reading one.

Closing a file. Closing a write file or an append file causes the records in the buffer to be written. Closing any file releases the buffer and file data area used to process the file. The BASIC statement is very simple:

900 CLOSE #1

Input/Output

This statement closes file #1. The **fclose( )** function closes a file in a C program:

if ((x = fclose(f1)) != NULL)

The file identifier is the only argument of function **fclose( )**. When you put the function call in an **if** statement, you can include a block of statements that are executed if the file doesn't close satisfactorily. Swapping disks while a program is executing causes an error when you try to close the file (among other problems). You may or may not be able to recover at this point by swapping the disks back.

You might want to read an MS-DOS sequential file written by MS-BASIC or some other MS-DOS program. Each record of this type of file is a variable-length record consisting of ASCII characters with newline and carriage return characters indicating the ends of the records. Declare a string long enough to contain the longest record, plus one character for the null character. Then use an **fgets( )** function to read the entire string. You can write a function to scan the string for the commas (or other characters) that separate the data items in the record. Function **fgets( )** leaves the newline character at the end of the string; if you write the record with function **fputs( )**, you must remove the newline character because function **fputs( )** supplies one.

Random File Operations

Like the random file of BASIC, the random file of the standard I/O functions is a file that consists of fixed-length records. The record can contain ASCII characters only, or it can include numeric variables in their internal format, which can save space on the file. In general, the standard I/O library provides a means of doing everything you can do with a BASIC file. You have more flexibility, but you must be more specific.

Opening a file. The BASIC OPEN statement for a random file looks like this:

200 OPEN "R", #1, "B:ACCOUNTS", 60

This statement opens file "B:ACCOUNTS" as file #1, a random file of 60-character records.

A declarator similar to that required for a sequential file is required for a random file:

FILE *rfl;

133

Chapter 9

The declarator does not have to be separate from declarators for other files. All files can be declared in one declarator statement. Once the file has been declared, call function **fopen( )** to open the file:

if ((rfl = fopen("B:ACCOUNTS","wb+")) == NULL)
 printf("Can't open input file");

Notice that the only difference between the call to open this file and the call to open a sequential file is the mode string. This string, consisting of **wb+**, means "write update." However, two other modes also apply to random files:

rb+
read update
ab+
append update

All three update modes allow both reading and writing. Typically, random file records are read and written without closing and reopening the file to change modes. If your program only reads or writes, you can use the **rb**, **wb**, or **ab** mode.

Even though they all allow both reading and writing, the three update modes are not interchangeable. Use **wb+** when you first open the file; like **wb**, it deletes any existing file with the same name. The file must be available if you use **rb+**; use it to read, modify, or add to an existing file. When you use **ab+**, you can read any record in the file, but you can write records only at the end of the file. It's really not of much value for a random file.

For random file operations using records that consist entirely of strings, omit the *b*; use **r+** for read update, **w+** for write update, and **a+** for append update.

Defining a record. The FIELD statement of BASIC defines a record for a random file:

100 FIELD #1, 25 AS NAM$, 25 AS ADDRESS$, 4 AS DUE$

This statement applies to the file opened as file #1. It reserves 25 character positions for variable NAM$, 25 character positions for variable ADDRESS$, and 4 character positions for variable DUE$. By using function MKS$, you can store any single-precision variable as DUE$.

Use a structure to define the record in C as you did for a sequential file:

Input/Output

```
struct rrec {
  char nam[25];
  char address[25];
  float due;
} account;
```

In the BASIC program, the record definition is tied directly to the file. In C, the structure is not tied directly to the file. The structure template can be used (tag *rrec*) for other structures, and members of structure *account* can be accessed like members of any other structure in the program. Define the structure ahead of the start of the *main()* function, making it accessible to the other functions also.

In a BASIC program, it is sometimes necessary to store a real number like DUE$ as a string of ASCII characters instead of in the internal format for a real number. This can happen if the file must be sent by a telephone line; sometimes the internal format of a number is taken as a control character by the modem. To do this, declare all structure members as strings. You must be sure to make the member large enough to include the number in string form plus a null character.

Writing a record. In BASIC, you use an INPUT statement to read the name and the LSET statement to move it to the record buffer:

300 INPUT "Name: ",NAM1$
310 LSET NAM$ = NAM1$

In C, you can read the name directly into the structure, like this:

printf("Name: ");
gets(account.nam);

Use similar statements to place the address and amount due into the structure. Then you are ready to write the structure in a specified record, perhaps using a hash code of the name as the record number (see Chapter 8).

BASIC uses a PUT statement to write a random file record:

350 PUT #1, N

This statement writes a record to file #1. The record number is N. The standard I/O library has no equivalent of the BASIC PUT statement, so you must write one, using the functions that are available. The call is:

Chapter 9

```
if ((x = put(rf1,&account,n)) != 0)
printf("Random file write error %d.\n",x);
```

Argument *rf1* is the file identifier, *account* is the record structure, and *n* is the record number. The function call is in an **if** statement that displays an error message when the function returns an error code. Function **put( )** calls three standard I/O functions:

```
put(fp,record,num) /* Write Random Record */
FILE *fp;
struct rrec *record;
int num;
{
long strec;
int code, rlen, i;

rlen = sizeof *record;
strec = num * rlen;
if ((code = fseek(fp,strec,0)) != NULL) {
   if ((code = fseek(fp,0L,2)) != NULL)
      return (-1);
   while ((code = fseek(fp,strec,0)) != NULL)
      for (i = 0; i < rlen; i++)
         fputc('\0',fp);
   }
if ((code = fwrite(record,rlen,1,fp)) == 1)
   return (0);
else
   return (1);
}
```

Function **put( )** uses operator **sizeof** to set variable *rlen* to the length of the records in this file, and multiplies the record number *num* by *rlen* to compute the position in the file at which the record is written. This position may be immediately following the last record in the file, within the current limits of the file, or beyond the end of the file. In either of the first two cases, the **fseek( )** function returns a NULL and function **put( )** calls function **fwrite( )** to write the record.

The **fseek( )** function is a standard I/O function that is required for random file operations. It sets the position in the file for the next operation at a point beyond the start of the file, relative to the current file position, or ahead of the end of the file. When the requested position is ahead of or at the end of the file, function **fseek( )** changes the current position to the

Input/Output

requested position and returns a 0, or NULL. When the position is beyond the end of the file, the function doesn't alter the current position, and returns a -1.

The first argument for the **fseek( )** function is the file identifier. The second is the value added to the reference point to determine the new current position. This value must be type **long**; it represents a number of *bytes*. The third argument is the mode: 0, 1, or 2. Mode 0 adds the value of the second argument to the start of the file. In other words, the second argument is an absolute position in the file; the argument must be positive. Mode 1 adds the value of the second argument to the current position in the file. In this case, the second argument is a position relative to the current position, positive or negative. Mode 2 adds the value of the second argument to the end-of-file position. The second argument is a position relative to the end-of-file. It's usually zero and cannot be positive. Mode 2 is not available on all computers (although it is available on all those that use MS-DOS). This example uses mode 2; you might have to modify it for use on some computers.

If the position is beyond the end of the file, function **put( )** must find the end of the file and write null records up to the requested position, then write the record. The second call to function **fseek( )**, with 0L and 2 as the last two arguments, finds the end of the file. The **while** loop writes null records until the **fseek( )** function returns a NULL. Then function **put( )** calls function **fwrite( )** to write the record. Notice that a seek error returns a code of -1, a write error that occurs while writing the record returns a code of 1, and a successful write operation returns a code of 0.

Reading a record. The BASIC statement that reads a random file record is the GET statement:

450 GET #1, N

This statement reads record N of random file #1. The same FIELD statement applies to both the PUT and GET operations. The standard I/O library has no equivalent of the GET statement, so you must write your own. Here's the call:

```
if ((x = get(rfl,&account,n)) == EOF)
    printf("Record %d is not in the file.\n",n);
```

The **get( )** function is similar to the **put( )** function, but a bit less complicated:

Chapter 9

```
get(fp,record,num) /* Read Random Record */
FILE *fp;
struct rrec *record;
int num;
{
long strec;
int code, rlen, i;

rlen = sizeof *record;
strec = num * rlen;
if ((code = fseek(fp,strec,0)) != NULL)
   return (EOF);
if ((code = fread(record,rlen,1,fp)) == 1)
   return (0);
else
   printf("Error reading record %d\n",num);
return (1);
}
```

When the **fseek( )** function returns a value other than NULL, the requested record is not within the limits of the file, and function **get( )** returns EOF. Otherwise, function **get( )** calls function **fread( )** to read the record. When the read operation is successful, function **get( )** returns 0. When the read operation is not successful, the function assumes that a read error has occurred and returns 1.

The error messages that the examples include can be a bit misleading. For example, if your file contains null records, the read operation gives no error indication when you read these records. If you want to reject them, you must include a statement in the calling function to test each record for valid contents. Also, the error returned by the read operation can be the end-of-file instead of an error. If it makes an important difference, use function **feof( )** to check for end-of-file.

Closing a random file is the same as closing a sequential file, both in BASIC and in C. Look in the subsection (above) on closing sequential files for details.

Printing

In general, I/O to other devices is very similar to sequential file operations except that the file specification in the call to function **fopen( )** is a device name. The device name for the printer is PRN:.

Before you can print, you must include the FILE declarator statement:

Input/Output

FILE *pr;

This statement can be combined with a FILE declarator statement for your files, but if printing is the only I/O operation in your program, you need this statement as it is. To open the printer, use a call to function **fopen( )**:

if((pr = fopen("PRN:","w")) == NULL)
  printf("Can't open the printer.\n");

The principal difference between this statement and a statement to open a file is that you use the device name instead of the filename. Mode **w** is the only mode that applies to the printer.

The LPRINT statement of BASIC prints a line on your printer:

500 LPRINT "BALANCE $";BAL

This statement prints the string constant BALANCE $ and the numeric variable BAL. The C equivalent is a call to the **fprintf( )** function:

fprintf(pr,"BALANCE $%.2f\n",bal);

To print a string, you can use the **fputs( )** function:

fputs("Printing in C is easy\n",pr);

When you have printed all the information that needs to be printed, you should close the printer:

fclose(pr);

An Illustration

This example program accepts lines of characters you type in and prints them on your printer, translating control characters into the control strings that cause special printing. It works with all printers that follow the Epson standard for dot-matrix printers (including the Star and the IBM 80 CPS Matrix and Graphics printers) which print italics, wide characters, and emphasized characters. You may have to change the translation constants for other printers. See your printer manual for the control strings for your printer.

Type control characters by pressing and holding the CTRL key while you press the key for the accompanying letter. The program translates the following control characters:

CTRL-Q   Begin italics
CTRL-W   Begin wide characters

Chapter 9

CTRL-E   Begin emphasized characters
CTRL-R   Return to normal characters

This program will compile, link, and run.

```c
#include <stdio.h>
/* Translation constants for Epson standard printers */
#define CC1 '\x11'
#define ITALICS "\x1B4\0"
#define CC2 '\x17'
#define WIDE "\x0E\0"
#define CC3 '\x05'
#define EMPH "\x1BE\0"
#define CC4 '\x12'
#define NORM "\x1B5\x1BF\x14\0"
/* End of translation constants */
FILE *pr;
main( ) /* Print with special characters */
{
static char line[100];
if((pr = fopen("PRN:","w")) == NULL) {
  printf("Can't open printer.\n");
  exit( );
  }
getts(line);
while(strlen(line) > 1) {
  fprintf(pr,"%s",line);
  getts(line);
  }
fputc('\n',pr);
fclose(pr);
}
getts(str) /* Input line replacing control characters */
char str[ ];
{
int c, i;
i = 0;
while (i < 94) {
  switch (c = getchar( )) {
    case CC1 :
    str[i] = '\0';
    strcat(str,ITALICS);
    i = strlen(str);
    break;
    case CC2 :
    str[i] = '\0';
```

Input/Output

```
            strcat(str,WIDE);
            i = strlen(str);
            break;
        case CC3 :
            str[i] = '\0';
            strcat(str,EMPH);
            i = strlen(str);
            break;
        case CC4 :
            str[i] = '\0';
            strcat(str,NORM);
            i = strlen(str);
            break;
        case '\n' :
            str[i++] = '\n';
            str[i] = '\0';
            return;
        default :
            str[i++] = c;
        }
    }
    return;
}
```

The first part of the program consists of compiler control lines, described in the next chapter. The **#include** line is required in a program that performs file I/O. The **#define** lines assign symbolic names to the control characters and to the corresponding control strings. Specifically, *CC1* is CTRL-Q, *CC2* is CTRL-W, *CC3* is CTRL-E, and *CC4* is CTRL-R. To change either the control characters or the strings, change only the **#define** lines; the program remains correct.

The executable part of the program begins by opening the printer and displays an error message when the operation fails. Next, the program calls function **getts( )** to get a string and perform any required translations. The **while** loop prints a string and gets another as long as you continue to type in strings. When you press RETURN instead of typing a string, the program closes the printer and terminates.

The **getts( )** function sets index *i* to 0 and accepts characters as long as there is space in the line for another character. The **switch** statement reads the characters you type and looks for the control characters defined by *CC1*, *CC2*, *CC3*, and *CC4*. When you type one of these characters, the statement calls

141

Chapter 9

function **strcat( )** to add the appropriate control string to the current string and function **strlen( )** to set variable *i* to the correct value. When you type any other character except a newline, the statement adds the character to the line. When you press RETURN, the statement adds a newline character and a null character and returns.

This chapter has shown you a few of the I/O functions in the standard I/O library supplied by Lattice. These functions are typical of the rest and of those in the standard libraries of other compilers. They give you more flexibility in I/O operations, but you must use them carefully. The Lattice C Compiler doesn't check arguments of functions; if you have an error in an argument, you find out about it when your program fails.

Now that you know how to perform I/O operations in the C language, you're nearly done. But don't skip the next chapter on compiler control lines. They can be very useful, if you know how to use them.

Chapter 10
Compiler Control Lines

Chapter 10
Compiler Control Lines

Compiler control lines are lines of your program that change your source program before it is compiled. They are also called *preprocessor directives,* because they are sometimes performed by a program called a *preprocessor.* In any case, these lines always begin with a number sign (#), which *must* be in column 1, and they don't have a semicolon (;) at the end.

Not all C compilers include a preprocessor; Lattice C does not. The compiler processes the compiler control lines along with the statements of the program. But the concept of a preprocessor will help you understand how compiler control lines work.

The preprocessor reads the source program before the source program goes to the compiler and looks for control lines that begin with a number sign (#). Each of these lines specifies something to be done to the source program. As the preprocessor continues to read the source program, it applies the commands in any command lines to the statements of the program. After reading the entire program, the preprocessor passes the modified source file to the compiler. Where the compiler itself performs the preprocessor operations (Lattice C, for instance), the compiler does the preprocessor processing ahead of compilation. The result is the same as if a separate preprocessor had modified the source file. When you see the word *preprocessor* anywhere in the rest of this chapter, remember that it means either a separate preprocessor or the preprocessor portion of the compiler.

Many compiler control lines are placed ahead of the C statements, but you can put a control line anywhere in the source program. It becomes effective at the point at which it appears in the program and remains in effect for the remainder of the source file.

Chapter 10

The compiler control lines consist of two groups: lines that directly alter the program and lines that conditionally alter the program. The first group consists of:

#include
#define
#undef

The conditional group includes:

#if
#ifdef
#ifndef
#else
#endif

include

The **#include** control line is used in most C source files. This line causes the preprocessor to read the named file as part of the source program. The lines and statements in that file become part of the source file, inserted in place of the **#include** control line. You've seen this line in several example programs in this book:

#include <stdio.h>

File **stdio.h** is one of several *header* files supplied with your compiler. It contains control lines and declarator statements that you need to perform I/O successfully with the standard I/O functions. The example control line effectively makes the contents of file **stdio.h** a part of your source program.

The library supplied with the Lattice C Compiler includes header files required for several of the functions. Using **#include** lines, you can include one or more of these header files, according to what your program needs. The descriptions of the functions that require header files tell you which header file(s) to include.

When the functions you write for your program are on more than one file, the external data items are usually required by functions in all files. The best way to provide the declarator statements for these items to all files is to put them in a header file and use an **#include** control line in each file. It is not necessary to use the .h extension for your header file, but using it helps you remember what the file is for. Here's an example of the control line to read header file B:PROG.H:

Compiler Control Lines

```
#include "b:prog.h"
```

Notice that this example uses quotation marks to enclose the file specification instead of angle brackets. With Lattice C, the two forms of the **#include** control line are interchangeable. However, with other implementations of C, use the quotation marks when the header file is in the same directory as the source files; use angle brackets when the header file is in a standard location for header files. When you use quotation marks, the preprocessor searches for the specified file in the current directory first, then in the standard locations. When you use angle brackets, only the standard locations are searched.

define

The **#define** control line has two uses. The first use is to assign a value to a *symbolic constant* in your program. The programs in this book show several examples of this use of the **#define** control line. Here's another:

```
#define YEAR 1986
```

If you write a program that requires the number of the current year in various places, you should use a symbolic constant. If you write the actual number as a constant in each statement that requires the value, you will be busy early every January changing all those statements and testing your program to be sure you found them all. If you use a symbolic constant, all you have to do is change the value in the **#define** statement and recompile your program. The preprocessor quietly (and consistently) plugs in the constant in place of the symbol before compiling the program.

Another advantage of using symbolic constants for most of the constants in your program is that the symbols are more meaningful when you read your program than the equivalent numbers would be. You'll be surprised how quickly you forget what you were doing when you wrote the program. Use symbols and comments liberally to help you find those problems that come up after the program has been working for several months.

The value of a symbolic constant in a **#define** line doesn't have to be a numeric value. The preprocessor substitutes just about anything for the symbolic constant. One limitation imposed by the Lattice C Compiler for the substituted

Chapter 10

string is that it cannot contain a **sizeof** operator. Here's an example of the different things you can do:

```
#define STOP printf("Stop. Press RETURN to continue"); \
   getchar( )
```

Notice the back slash character; it continues the substitution on the next line. To use this in your program, write a statement like this:

```
STOP;
```

The preprocessor replaces *STOP* with the rest of the characters on the command line. This provides a pause in your program similar to that provided by a STOP statement in BASIC. There's an important difference, though. You cannot type in commands while you're stopped. This example is useful to allow you to change forms on the printer or to place a different disk in a drive.

This is an example of the other use of the **#define** control line: to define a *macro*. STOP is the macro name; when the preprocessor finds the macro name in the source program, it replaces the macro name with the macro. This macro becomes a portion of the program; it can include one or more variables, like this:

```
#define DISPLAY(v) printf("The result is %d.\n",v)
```

The *v* in parentheses following *DISPLAY* is the variable for the macro. Notice that it also appears in the macro. Don't include a space anywhere in the macro name, not even ahead of the left parenthesis. The preprocessor uses the space to identify the end of the macro name. If, for instance, you put a space between *DISPLAY* and the left parenthesis, the macro name would be *DISPLAY*, with no variable defined. In your program, call the macro like this:

```
DISPLAY(length);
```

The preprocessor uses the variable in the macro call by plugging it into the macro instead of *v*. In this example, *length* is the variable used in the call to function **printf( )**. Variable *length* must have been declared as an integer. You can use an expression having an integer value in place of *length* in the macro call. The expression replaces *v* in that case.

A macro can include more than one variable. For instance,

```
#define NEWSQR(a,b) (a + b / a) / 2
```

Compiler Control Lines

This macro computes an approximation of a square root of a number, where *a* is the initial approximation and *b* is the number. It can be used in a **for** loop:

```
for(x1=r;abs(x−x1) > .0001;) {
  x = x1;
  x1 = NEWSQR(x,y);
}
```

To use this example, assign an estimate of the square root of *y* to *r*, and a different value to *x*. Then perform the loop. Each time you compute a new value of *x1*, you add *x* to the quotient of *y* divided by *x* and divide the sum by 2. The value of *x1* approaches the square root of *y*. When the difference between the two most recent approximations is less than 0.0001, you have the square root accurate to three decimal places. By the way, if you have a square root function in a library supplied with your compiler, it's a better way to figure square roots than this.

Take another look at the macro. Remember that when you call the macro, the macro name is replaced by:

(x + y/x) / 2

The computations are performed when you run the program, and using numeric variables for *x* and *y*, the result is correct. But look what happens if the second variable is replaced by an expression, as in this call:

x1 = NEWSQR(x,y+2);

When the program is compiled, the assignment statement becomes:

x1 = (x + y + 2/x) / 2

You'll never get close to the square root of *y* + 2 that way. But the fix is easy:

#define NEWSQR(a,b) (a + (b)/a) / 2

Using this macro in the problem statement results in this assignment statement:

x1 = (x + (y + 2)/x) / 2

This particular macro will work with any items that are very likely to be used with it. But the rule is to use parentheses around each variable of the macro definition and around the entire definition. Thus, the macro definition should be:

#define NEWSQR(a,b) (((a) + (b)/(a)) / 2)

Chapter 10

Do not use the ++ or −− operator in a macro call. Here's an example of what can happen. The macro definition is:

#define CUBE(x) ((x) * (x) * (x))

Calling the macro in a statement like this causes the problem:

n = CUBE(++b);

When the program is compiled, this statement becomes:

n = ((++b) * (++b) * (++b));

The answer is not going to be correct. Don't use a function call in a macro call, either.

Have you noticed that a function call and a macro call look very much alike? This can be confusing, because a function and a macro have important differences. The function appears once in your program, no matter how often you call it. Each call causes the program to branch to the function, passing the required parameters to the function. On the other hand, each macro call causes the preprocessor to plug in the constant, string, or expression in place of the macro name. The program is exactly as it would have been if you had not used a macro, but had written the constant, string, or expression in each statement instead of the macro call.

Sometimes you can use either a macro or a function; either does the job adequately. Other times you must use a function instead of a macro to avoid the problems that macros have. Or you have an operation that must work for either integers or real numbers. You would need one function for the integers and another for the real numbers; use a macro in this case. But often you have a choice.

If there are many calls to the macro, the program that uses the macro needs more memory than the one that uses the function. However, the program that uses the function runs more slowly. Sometimes you need all the memory space you can get; use a function. Other times your program has time constraints; use a macro.

Several of the header files in the library supplied with Lattice C Version 2.14 and 2.15 contain macros. The library also contains some functions that you can use instead of some of these macros. Specifically, the following calls in your program can call either a macro or a function:

Compiler Control Lines

Macro	Header File
abs(x)	stdio.h
isalpha(c)	ctype.h
isupper(c)	ctype.h
islower(c)	ctype.h
isdigit(c)	ctype.h
isspace(c)	ctype.h
isalnum(c)	ctype.h
iscntrl(c)	ctype.h
toupper(c)	ctype.h
tolower(c)	ctype.h

When you compile your program and the macro has been defined (that is, the appropriate header file is included), the compiler plugs in the macro definition and the function is not used. But if the macro has not been defined, the compiler puts code in the object file to call the function. Then, when you link the program (see Chapter 11), the LINK utility gets the function from the library. Including the proper header file gives you the macro instead of the function. To get the function, leave out the header file. But there can be a problem: You cannot omit header file **stdio.h** if your program performs file I/O. The next section provides a solution.

undef

The **#undef** control line removes a previously defined constant or macro. Here's an example:

#undef STOP

This control line removes macro *STOP* defined in a preceding example. You very seldom need to do this, because having the macro definition available does no harm. If the macro isn't called, your program will be the same whether the macro is defined or not.

One case where you need this control line is when a required header file contains a macro having the same name as a function that you need to call. For example, if your program includes header file **stdio.h**, you might need this control line (following the **include** <stdio.h> line):

#undef abs

Macro **abs** is now undefined and calls to **abs** call function **abs( )**, but don't do this unless you're sure you need to. Macro **abs** works for either integers or real numbers; function **abs( )**

Chapter 10

works for integers only. The library includes function **fabs( )** for real numbers.

When you use a **#define** control line that has the same macro name as a control line already in effect, the new definition applies. You can remove the new definition and restore the previous one with an **undef** control line. This could be required if you defined a special macro with the same name as a standard macro to use in a part of the program. Put a control line defining the new macro ahead of the first call:

```
#define min(a,b) ((a)<=(b)?(a):(a)-(b))
```

This macro replaces the standard macro that returns either a or b, whichever is least. This macro returns a if a is less than b. It returns the difference if a is greater than b. If you later need the standard macro in your program, use this control line:

```
#undef min(a,b)
```

The standard macro is available again. You should avoid this kind of programming because it makes understanding your program unnecessarily difficult. You can usually use a different macro name for the new macro. Remember, you could be the one confused by this programming double-talk when you have to fix the program after you have forgotten what you did.

Conditional Compiling

The *conditional compiler control lines* do for the compilation process what **if** statements do in your program. They cause different results according to the value of an expression. Specifically, conditional compiler control lines cause the compiler to select parts of the program to compile. The condition for selecting can be the value of a symbolic constant, or whether the constant has been defined. The optional part of the program can include control lines, C statements, or both.

if and endif

The **if** control line begins the conditional portion of your program, and the **endif** portion marks the end of the conditional portion. Here's an example:

```
#if PRINT == 1
if((pr = fopen("PRN:","w")) == NULL) {
   printf("Can't open printer.\n");
```

Compiler Control Lines

```
    exit( );
}
#endif
```

You can write a program that you can compile either to print error messages or to display them on the screen. By defining constant PRINT equal to 1, you cause the compiler to process statements that open the printer. When you don't define constant PRINT, the compiler ignores these statements.

else

The **#else** control line marks the end of a conditional portion of the program and begins an alternative portion. In other words, you use it between an **#if** and an **#endif** to provide a choice between two sets of control lines or statements. In the preceding example, you need different functions for printing and displaying messages. You can use this:

```
#if PRINT == 1
fprintf(pr,"Read error, file %s.\n",filnam);
#else
printf("Read error, file %s.\n",filnam);
#endif
```

By defining PRINT appropriately, you can compile a program that prints error messages instead of displaying them.

ifdef and ifndef

The **#ifdef** control line inserts a portion of the program when a constant is defined. It's like the **#if** control line except that it doesn't compare the value of the constant to anything. You could have used this control line in the two previous examples:

```
#ifdef PRINT
```

Those examples would work the same way as long as you defined PRINT (any value) for printing messages and did not define PRINT for displaying messages. The **#ifndef** control line is the negative of **ifdef**. You could replace the **#if** control lines in the same two examples with this:

```
#ifndef DISPLAY
```

With this change, the program would compile for printing when it didn't define constant DISPLAY, and it would compile for displaying when it defined DISPLAY.

Chapter 10

Conditional compiling can produce two or more versions of a program from one source program with a minimum of additional effort. But the example program shows what is possibly the most practical use of conditional compiling.

An Illustration

When you debug a C program, you can use some of the same techniques you have been using to debug your BASIC programs. But because the C programs are compiled instead of being interpreted, you must use the techniques differently. Conditional compiling can be a big help.

In a BASIC program, you can insert a STOP statement at a critical point in your program and run the program. When the "Break" message is displayed, you can type in a PRINT command to see if key variables have the correct values. Displaying these values helps you to close in on errors.

In a C program, you have to put the debugging statements in the program. You have to put them at critical points and remove them and recompile after the program is debugged. When an error turns up later, you may have to put some back in, recompile, and run the program again. Conditional compiling can insert and remove those statements easily and consistently. Just change the value of a symbolic constant and recompile.

Plan your debugging as you write your program. Assign a symbolic constant for the debug mode. (If you use Lattice C, do not use DEBUG; the compiler uses it for *its* debug mode.) Use appropriate levels of debugging and assign a value for each. In the example, when constant DEBUGG has a value of 3, the program displays all debugging information. A value of 2 causes the program to display debugging information for functions **record( )** and **print( )** only. Setting DEBUGG to 1 displays debugging messages in function **print( )** only.

Changing the debugging mode involves changing only the **#define** control line that defines DEBUGG. Removing that line turns off all debugging. The compiled object code doesn't have even a vestige of the debugging code. But it's all in the source file, ready to turn on with a **#define** line if it is needed. (See Chapter 11 for more complete debugging information.)

This example program maintains a register of the checks you write on a sequential file. It prints a list of your checks

Compiler Control Lines

when you need it. It will compile, link, and run. Look it over, and see how the debugging works:

```
#include <stdio.h>
#define DEBUGG 3
FILE *pr, *fi;
struct {
   char date[15];
   char name[50];
   float amt;
   } check;
main(argc,argv) /* Check File Program */
int argc;
char *argv[ ];
{
int in;
if(argc < 2) {
   printf("I need a filename. Try again.\n");
   exit( );
   }
printf("%33sCHECK RECORDER\n\n\n"," ");
printf("%20sTo help you keep track of your checks.\n"," ");
printf("%20sChoose what you want to do:\n\n"," ");
printf("%23s1 Add checks to the file.\n"," ");
printf("%23s2 Print check register.\n\n\n"," ");
do {
   printf("%20sType 1 or 2 and press RETURN, please: "," ");
   if ((in = getchar( )) == '1') {
#if DEBUGG == 3
   printf("Record %s\n",argv[1]);
#endif
   record (argv[1]);
   }
   else if (in == '2') {
#if DEBUGG == 3
   printf("Print %s\n",argv[1]);
#endif
   print (argv[1]);
   }
   putchar('\n');
   }
while (in < '1' || in > '2');
}
record(file) /* Write a record for a check */
char file[ ];
{
int x, m, n = 1;
```

155

Chapter 10

```c
if((fi = fopen(file,"ab")) == NULL) {
  printf("Can't open file.\n");
  exit ();
  }
do {
  printf("Check No. %d.\n\n",n++);
  printf("Type date: (no. of month/no. of day/");
  printf("last 2 digits of year) ");
  while (getchar() != '\n')
      ;
  gets(&check.date);
  printf("Paid to: ");
  gets(&check.name);
  printf("Amount: $");
  scanf("%f",&check.amt);
  printf("Another check? (Y or N) ");
  x = getche();
  putchar('\n');
#if DEBUGG > 1
  printf("%-18s%-50s%10.2f\n",check.date,check.name,
      check.amt);
#endif
  if ((m = fwrite(&check,sizeof check,1,fi)) < 1)
      printf("Error writing check no. %d.\n",n);
  }
while (x == 'Y' || x == 'y');
if((m = fclose(fi)) != NULL)
  printf("File doesn't want to close.\n");
return;
}
print(fname) /* Print check register */
char fname[ ];
{
int n;
float total;
if ((fi = fopen(fname,"rb")) == NULL) {
  printf("Can't open file.\n");
  exit();
  }
if ((pr = fopen("PRN:","w")) == NULL) {
  printf("Can't open printer.\n");
  exit();
  }
total = 0;
while (feof(fi) == 0) {
```

Compiler Control Lines

```
    if ((n = fread(&check,sizeof check,1,fi)) < 1) {
      if(ferror(fi) != 0)
        printf("Error reading file.\n");
      break;
      }
    total += check.amt;
#if DEBUGG > 0
    printf("%-18s%-50s%10.2f\n",check.date,check.name,
      check.amt);
    printf("%12.2f\n",total);
#endif
    fprintf(pr,"%-18s%-48s $%10.2f\n",check.date,check.name,
      check.amt);
  }
  fprintf(pr,"Total amount of checks:%42c%$12.2f\n",' ',total);
  if((n = fclose(pr)) != NULL)
    printf("Printer doesn't want to close.\n");
  if((n = fclose(fi)) != NULL)
    printf("File doesn't want to close.\n");
  return;
}
```

The example program gets the file specification from the command line, using a technique described in Chapter 4. The example in Chapter 4 got a number you typed following the program name. Using the technique to get a file specification is more typical. If you fail to type in a specification, the program displays an error message and quits. If you type in more than one file specification, the program uses the first one and ignores the rest.

The program either stores the information about your checks in a file or lists the checks on the printer. It also totals the amounts of the checks as it lists them. It's primarily intended to show the use of conditional compiling for debugging; you can add other statements to make it more useful.

The next chapter tells you how to compile, link, and debug your programs. You may have already looked ahead so you could try some examples.

Chapter 11
Finishing Touches

Chapter 11
Finishing Touches

Now that you have learned about C and its accessories, it's time to learn how to run the compiler and other utilities that help you develop C programs. It's time to get your programs up and running, to start getting some useful software.

The operation information in this chapter is for the Lattice C Compiler and utilities and doesn't apply to other compilers, except in a general way. The same is true of error message information. Information about the Microsoft LINK utility applies to the linking of most software for the IBM PC and similar computers. However, the general information about compiling, debugging, and linking should help you even if you have a different compiler.

Completing Your Program
The MS-DOS text editor EDLIN, which is typical of line-oriented text editors, is intended for writing source files. Most word processors have a mode that is appropriate for writing source code. Use whichever works best for you, and assign .C as the extension in the file specification. You are now ready to compile the program.

For the discussion that follows and the remainder of this chapter, it is assumed that the disk containing your source code is in drive B and that the C compiler disk or linker disk with the C libraries (whichever is appropriate) is in drive A.

If you're using a single-drive system, you will need to swap disks. Whenever you're prompted for drive A, insert your C compiler disk or linker disk with libraries (whichever is appropriate) into your drive. When prompted for drive B, insert the disk with the C source code.

Compiling Your Program
The Lattice C Compiler consists of two programs (called phases). Phase 1 (LC1) reads the source file, detects errors in

Chapter 11

your code, and translates the program into an intermediate code, which it writes to a file. Phase 2 (LC2) reads this file and translates the code into machine language for the 8086 microprocessor.

To run phase 1 of the compiler, type the following with your C compiler disk in drive A and the disk with your source code in drive B and press RETURN:

LC1 B:*filename*

The *filename* is the file specification of the source file, minus the extension. The extension must be .C, and it should not be typed in. LC1 displays the program name and version information, followed by error messages for any errors the compiler detects. LC1 also writes the intermediate file. When LC1 terminates with errors, it deletes the intermediate file. This keeps you from running LC2 with an intermediate file that contains errors.

LC1 has several options that you can specify, but most programs can be compiled without specifying any options. Some of the options are described in subsequent sections of this chapter. For a complete list of available options, see the Lattice C Compiler manual.

When LC1 completes with no error messages, you are ready to run LC2. Type the following with your C compiler disk in drive A and the disk with your source code in drive B and press RETURN:

LC2 B:*filename*

The *filename* is the same file specification you used to run LC1. LC2 displays the program name and version number, and writes the object file. You should not see any error messages from LC2; any error message you might see is a compiler problem, not a problem in your program. When LC2 completes, you have an object file of machine instructions ready for linking.

Linking Your Program

Every C program calls some library functions, whether you explicitly call a library function or not. These library functions must be linked with the object file written by LC2 to provide an integrated executable program. MS-DOS utility LINK does the job nicely.

Finishing Touches

You may not know that you have LINK on your system disk, because the MS-DOS manuals supplied with your computer may not tell you about it. Texas Instruments, for one, did not provide any information about LINK with the original MS-DOS documentation for the TI Professional. But if you display the directory (DIR command) of the system disk, you can see LINK.EXE there, ready for you to use.

The LINK utility reads your object file and identifies the library functions that it calls. Then it searches the library file(s) to find the object modules for these functions. It integrates the object modules you need with your object file and writes the executable file (using extension .EXE). If the LINK utility doesn't display any error messages, your program is complete, ready for you to debug.

(Please note: the description below instructs you to use files CS.OBJ, LCS.LIB, and LCMS.LIB. Later versions of the Lattice C manual instruct you to copy and change the names of certain files based on the memory model you want to use. There are four memory models: S, D, P, and L. The filenames on the Lattice C disks append the model type to the filename. Thus, page 3 of the Lattice C Compiler manual 2.15A tells you to copy CS.OBJ to your linker disk as C.OBJ, LCS.LIB as LC.LIB, and so forth. In the examples below, it is assumed that you have *not* renamed these files and are using the S memory model. If you have changed the filenames, you should substitute the filenames you have on your disk. For instance LINK CS... should be LINK C..., and libraries LCS and LCMS should be LC and LCM.)

To link your program, place a disk with LINK.EXE and libraries in drive A and the disk with your source code in drive B, type the following, and press RETURN:

LINK CS+B:*filename*,**B:***fsa*,,*libraries*

Module CS contains the object code that builds **argv[ ]** (the array of command line strings) and sets **argc** to the number of strings in the array. The *filename* must be the same file specification you used for LC1 and LC2. The *fsa* is the file specification (except for the extension) for the executable file. For convenience, it should be the same as the file specification for LC1 and LC2, but you can use any valid filename. The extension, .EXE, is supplied by the LINK utility.

Chapter 11

If you're using Version 2.14 or 2.15 of Lattice C, or another version that has separate libraries for the mathematical functions, and your program doesn't contain any real numbers, use LCS for *libraries*. If your program includes any real numbers, use LCMS+LCS for *libraries*.

Running Your Program

Run your C language program as you would run any program under MS-DOS. Either place the disk on which the linking utility wrote the .EXE file in the default drive, or make the drive that contains that disk the default drive. Then type the filename of the program (without the extension) followed by any command line arguments and press RETURN.

Compiler Details

When you type the LC1 command as shown previously, the program displays any error messages on the screen. You can print them by pressing the PRINT key before you type the command. Or you can write them to a file by typing the LC1 command like this:

LC1 >B:PROG.ERL B:PROG

This command runs LC1, which writes error messages to file B:PROG.ERL and compiles source file B:PROG.C.

When header files or other files specified in **#include** control lines are in a different directory, use the **-i** option to identify the directory that contains these files:

**LC1 \SOURCE \PROG -i \HFILES **

This causes LC1 to compile the source file in directory SOURCE using header files in directory HFILES.

The examples shown previously have compiled the program for the S memory model, in which the program address space and the data address space are each limited to 64K bytes. This produces a more efficient program and provides enough space for most programs. For those of you who are familiar with the four segments of 8086/8088 machine language programs, the data segment, stack segment, and extra segment all begin at the same address in the S memory model. The code segment begins at a different address. See Appendix D for more information on segments and addresses.

Three other memory models are available for programs that need more than 64K bytes of program address space,

Finishing Touches

more than 64K bytes of data address space, or both. The P memory model provides more than 64K bytes of program address space and 64K bytes of data address space. The code segment begins at one address, and the data, stack, and extra segments all begin at another address in the P model, as in the S model. The D memory model provides 64K bytes of program address space and more than 64K bytes of data address space. The code, data, and stack segments each begin at a different address. The L memory model provides more than 64K bytes of program address space and more than 64K bytes of data address space. As in the D model, the three segments each begin at a different address. The P, D, and L models can address all available memory.

To use any of the additional memory models, you must compile and link your program for the required model. Specify one of the following options with the LC1 command:

−mP   For memory model P
−mD   For memory model D
−mL   For memory model L

For example:

LC1 B:PROG −mD

This example compiles source file B:PROG.C for memory model D. The program address space is limited to 64K. The rest of available memory is available for data.

Phase 2 of the compiler has few options. The one that you will probably use more than any other applies when you want to write the object file in a different directory. Here's an example:

**LC2 \SOURCE \PROG -o \FILES **

LC2 writes the object file for PROG in directory OFILES. The intermediate file was written by LC1 in directory \SOURCE\ with the source file.

LINK Utility Details

The MS-DOS LINK utility integrates object files and the library functions they call into a single executable module. The example linking command linked a single user object module for the S memory module. When you write and compile the functions for your program using several files, the link command looks like this:

LINK CS+B:PROG1+B:PROG2+B:PROG3,B:PROG,,LCMS+LCS

Chapter 11

The object modules for this program were written to three files: B:PROG1, B:PROG2, and B:PROG3. The plus signs (+) tell LINK that CS (for the S memory model), B:PROG1, B:PROG2, and B:PROG3 are to be integrated into one program, along with any library function modules they require. The executable module written by LINK is B:PROG.EXE. Libraries LCMS and LCS (for the S memory model) are searched for the required functions. Linking for the other memory models requires using a different C file and different library files:

CP, LCMP, and LCP for the P model
CD, LCMD, and LCD for the D model
CL, LCML, and LCL for the L model

Response File

When you have more than three object modules to link, use more plus signs and file specifications before the first comma. However, typing in a long command line can be tedious. You often have to link the program several times during the course of developing a program. One way to make linking easier is to write the linking file specifications in a file, called a *response file*. Then you can give the LINK utility the name of the file instead of a list of file specifications.

You can use EDLIN to write the link file, but it is easier to use the COPY command, like this:

COPY CON B:PROG.LNK

This tells the copy utility to copy keyboard input to file B:PROG.LNK. After you press RETURN, the computer waits for you to type in the information you want to put in the file. Begin by typing the names of the object modules to be linked, like this:

CS+B:PROG1+B:PROG2+B:PROG3

Then press RETURN and type the name of the executable file:

B:PROG

Press RETURN again. If you want a link map, type a filename here. The link map is described in a subsequent paragraph. Just press RETURN again for now. This provides a blank line in your file. Then type the library name(s):

LCMS+LCS

Finishing Touches

By the way, whether you type in the library names as part of the LINK command or as part of a response file, the order of the names is important. The two libraries contain different versions of some functions. If you are not using real numbers, you have a more efficient program when you use the versions of these functions in library LCS. But if you need the versions that use real numbers, you must place LCMS first, because LINK searches for functions from the first library file to the last, and stops when it finds a function with the required name. *The order of filenames in the responses to the LINK utility is usually critical.*

Press RETURN after you type the library names. Then press and hold the CTRL key as you press the Z key. This provides the end-of-file character, which causes the copy utility to write the file, display its message, and terminate. To link the program using the response file, type this:

LINK @B:PROG.LNK

The LINK utility runs, displaying the prompts with the responses from the response file plugged in. Slick, eh?

If you have more object module names than you can type on one line, type a plus sign (+) after the last one on the line and continue on the next line. Similarly, if you have more library names than fit on one line, use a plus sign at the end of the line and continue on the next line. The limit to the number of files you can have is larger than the number you are likely to type in.

Library Files

An object module and a library function module are linked in exactly the same way. The difference between object modules and library function modules with respect to linking is the manner in which they are specified to the linking utility. Each object module is explicitly named in the linking command. Object modules (even those in the library files) contain information that causes the linking utility to search for any required function not included in the module. The utility looks in the other object modules for the function. When the function is not in an object module, the utility searches the libraries in the order in which they are named. If the function cannot be found, the utility issues a "Not Resolved" message.

The linking utility does not know or care whether a library

Chapter 11

file you name is a standard library file. It can be any library file. You can put object modules that contain the functions you write in libraries of your own. The Lattice C Compiler package includes PLIB86, an object library manager. You can use it to build your own libraries and to examine and modify the standard libraries. To run the library manager, type:

PLIB86

When you press RETURN, PLIB86 runs, displaying its prompt. The following example shows the prompts and responses required to build a library file:

=> **BUILD B:MYLIB**
=> **FILE B:GET,B:PUT,B:FIX,B:PROG2;**

The BUILD command tells the library manager to build a library file named MYLIB.LIB on the disk in drive B:, including object modules B:GET, B:PUT, B:FIX, and B:PROG2 in the library. When PLIB86 finishes, it displays this message:

No fatal errors encountered

This library file contains the functions in the four object modules, all accessible by function name. Instead of listing one or more of these object modules in your link command, include the library name.

For more information about using PLIB86, refer to its manual included with your Lattice C Compiler manual.

Link Map

The link map written by the linking utility is very useful if you debug your program using the DEBUG program of MS-DOS. To obtain a map, place a file specification (without an extension) between the two adjacent commas in the command line or on the blank line of the response file. That is, the map file specification follows the executable file specification and precedes the library file specifications. Here's an example, which adds a file specification for the map to a link command example shown previously:

LINK CS+B:PROG1+B:PROG2+B:PROG3,B:PROG,B:PROG, LCMS+LCS /M

This example links four files, and writes executable file B:PROG.EXE and map file B:PROG.MAP. It is not necessary to use the same name for the executable file and for the map file, but doing so helps you identify the program to which the

168

Finishing Touches

map applies. The /M at the end of the command line is a switch that specifies the map option. You can write a map file without using the map option, but the map you get is limited.

The *link map* is written to the file you name. You can display it on the screen or print it. Figure 11-1 shows portions of the three sections of the link map. The first part lists the segments of the program, showing the starting and ending addresses, the length, and the class name of each. The linking utility uses the class names to arrange the segments for linking. This information is not of much value in debugging your program; it is all you get in the map file without the /M option.

The next section of the link map is an alphabetical list of the publics and the addresses corresponding to them. *Publics* are the names of functions and external data items. The last section lists these same publics and their addresses in address order.

Notice that the addresses consist of eight hexadecimal digits, with a colon separating four digits from the other four digits. The four digits to the left of the colon are the *segment address*. In the S memory model, the segment address for the code segment is 0000H, and the segment address for the data segment address is a larger number. The actual value depends on the size of the code segment. These addresses show you which items are functions (code segment addresses) and which are data items (data segment addresses). Because these addresses are relative to the address at which the program is loaded, they do not mean much other than that. The addresses you see when you use DEBUG are the actual runtime segment addresses. Appendix D discusses the segments and memory addressing for microprocessors.

The hexadecimal digits to the right of the colon are the *offset*, which is the address relative to the segment address. The offsets are the addresses you use in DEBUG commands. The main reason you want a link map is to obtain the offsets of functions and external data items.

Figure 11-1 lists only a few of the publics. The first time you look at a link map of one of your programs, you'll be surprised at the number of them. It will appear that the linking utility has included the entire library. When you compare the link maps of two different programs, though, you'll see that your program does not include the entire library. Here are the

169

Chapter 11

reasons for all the functions and data that you had no idea you needed:
1. Object module CS calls some functions and uses some data items that you are not concerned with.
2. Your program calls type conversion functions and some other functions without explicit function calls in your program.
3. The library functions call other library functions and use data items.
4. Some of the modules in the standard libraries contain several functions. You get all functions in the module when you call any one of them.

Figure 11-1. Link Map Example

Start	Stop	Length	Name	Class
00000H	00001H	0002H	BASE	PROG
00002H	050C1H	50C0H	PROG	PROG
050C2H	050C3H	0002H	TAIL	PROG
050D0H	05CA3H	0BD4H	DATA	DATA
05CB0H	05D2FH	0080H	STACK	DATA

Address	Publics by Name
0000:4AB2	ALLMEM
050D:068C	ARGC
050D:068E	ARGV
0000:50B0	BDOS
0000:4AC5	BLDMEM
0000:0002	C

Address	Publics by Value
0000:0002	C
0000:0203	XCOVF
0000:021F	XCEXIT
0000:0238	MAIN
0000:0394	CXM55
0000:03C8	SCANF

Program entry point at 0000:0002

Error Messages

Unless you're a very exceptional person, the first time you run LC1 you'll see some error messages. If you're like me, and you start with a large program, you will be *overwhelmed* with error

Finishing Touches

messages. Don't be discouraged. The only thing to do is correct the source program and get rid of the error messages, because you will get nowhere trying to run LC2 until LC1 terminates with no errors.

Figure 11-2 shows the error messages issued by LC1 for a 16-line source file. This source file is used in the OMD listing example, Figure 11-3. Look at the first error message, which applies to line 4. A separator, according to the error message information in Appendix A of the Lattice C manual, is a comma or semicolon. Here's line 4:

double pr, factor;

The comma and semicolon required in this statement are securely in place. Some other error in a previous statement must have made the compiler think that line 4 should contain an additional separator. A closer look at the program shows that the opening brace—following the *main( )* statement on line 3—is not there. After adding the brace and recompiling, *all* of the error messages went away. LC1 issued a different error message for an error on line 9. Omitting the opening brace had so disoriented LC1 that it was not able to identify the other error in the program correctly.

Figure 11-2. LC1 Error Message Example

```
B:PROG.C 4 Error 79: separator expected
B:PROG.C 6 Error 58: missing parenthesis
B:PROG.C 7 Error 79: separator expected
B:PROG.C 7 Error 77: identifier expected
B:PROG.C 8 Error 58: missing parenthesis
B:PROG.C 9 Error 79: separator expected
B:PROG.C 9 Error 77: identifier expected
B:PROG.C 10 Error 63: duplicate declaration of item "in"
B:PROG.C 10 Error 79: separator expected
B:PROG.C 11 Error 58: missing parenthesis
B:PROG.C 12 Error 79: separator expected
B:PROG.C 12 Error 77: identifier expected
B:PROG.C 14 Error 63: duplicate declaration of item "amt"
B:PROG.C 14 Error 79: separator expected
B:PROG.C 15 Error 58: missing parenthesis
B:PROG.C 16 Error 79: separator expected
B:PROG.C 16 Error 2: unexpected end of file
Execution terminated
```

Chapter 11

Based on conversations with others using Lattice C, I believe that the error messages are a real stumbling block to programmers using that compiler, particularly while they are learning the language. Many users cannot understand Kernighan and Ritchie. They buy books on C written for beginners. But the Lattice C error messages are written in the language of the "C Reference Manual," Appendix A, of Kernighan and Ritchie.

The language of the error messages is not the main problem, though. And in defense of Lattice C, part of the problem is unavoidable. For example, when you get a message that tells you that a semicolon is missing on line 12, the semicolon the message refers to is probably missing from line 11. That is because the compiler has no way of knowing where the semicolon should be. The semicolon tells the compiler where the statement ends. When the statement ends without a semicolon, the compiler must begin to read the next line before it can tell that a new statement has started somewhere without telling the compiler that the previous statement ended. There is no way the compiler can say for sure where the semicolon belongs. The examples in this book show each new statement starting on a separate line, but that is not a requirement; a statement can start at the end of a statement on the same line with it. When you see error 57, look to see if you omitted a semicolon in the line preceding the line on which the error was detected.

Similarly, adding or omitting a brace—{ or }—makes it impossible for the compiler to remain oriented properly with the statements of your program. The compiler cannot be sure what is wrong, so it tosses out error messages for several possible errors.

Because the computer has only one type of quotation mark (not an opening and a closing quotation mark like a typesetter has), an extra or omitted quotation mark can mean several possible errors. The compiler cannot tell which error you made.

However, the action the Lattice C Compiler takes when it detects some errors can force other errors further on in your program. For instance, when the compiler detects an undefined data item, it gives the item an integer value so that it is defined for the remainder of the program. If it is not intended to be an integer, and the compiler later detects that this item is

Finishing Touches

an integer where an item of another type should be, there's another error. Repeated error messages to the effect that the item is undefined would be easier to cope with.

Don't become discouraged with the number of error messages when you run LC1. In particular, don't be surprised if, when you correct one error, you get a different set of error messages. The reason for this is that by correcting the error, some of the previous error messages no longer apply, and the possible explanations of remaining errors have changed. It can be very frustrating, but it actually is valid for a whole new set of error messages to apply as a result of correcting an error.

Another explanation is that sometimes the number and nature of error messages cause the compiler to stop, displaying this message:

Execution terminated

The compiler has given up. After you have corrected these errors, the compiler may run to completion, or until it is again faced with a group of errors that it cannot unravel. During this rerun, the compiler examines statements it did not read previously, finding error messages it did not find before.

So much for LC1's problems with error detection. What do you do about errors? Here are some guidelines:

1. Analyze the error messages in the order in which the compiler detected them. Then when you correct one error, any additional errors related to the error you corrected will go away.
2. When the text of the error message does not seem to apply to the line specified in the message, check the syntax of the line carefully. Some errors result in seemingly unrelated error messages.
3. Check the syntax of the preceding lines. Several types of errors may not be detected on the line on which they occur.
4. After you have found the error that caused the first error message, correct the error. But before you attempt to compile the corrected program, carefully check the lines specified in subsequent error messages. Some of them will be the result of the error you have corrected, but some may be the result of other errors.

Fortunately, I haven't seen any error messages issued by LC2. If you do, you have a compiler problem. But the LINK

Chapter 11

utility issues error messages when it cannot find a file or cannot link the program properly. When the utility cannot find a file, either you have an error in the file specification or you have failed to do some required disk swapping. Just try again, using correct file specifications and disks.

The other type of linking error you may get is an unresolved reference. This happens when the LINK utility cannot find a function you have called. Check to be sure that you have included all required object and library files. This error also happens when you did not include a header file that contains a macro you used in the program. Normally, the preprocessor substitutes the macro for the macro call before compilation. When the header file is not available, the compiler assumes that the macro call is a function call. Macro and function calls look alike, and the compiler cannot know the names of all functions you might call. So it puts information in the object file asking the linking utility to find a function. When the linking utility fails to find a function by that name, you get the unresolved reference message. When it finds a function by that name, you may have a more difficult problem. The function may not do what the macro would have done, but you have no error message to tell you something is wrong.

Debugging Your Program

After you have corrected all the errors reported by the compiler and the LINK utility, you are ready to run your program. With all the errors corrected, the program should run, right? Yes, it should, and it usually does, at least to some extent. But computers are not smart. They don't do what you *meant* to tell them to do. They do only what you *tell* them to do. Sometimes the results are not what you intended. In that case, you must debug your program.

Chapter 10 describes the use of conditional compilation control lines to insert debugging statements. A **printf( )** statement at each strategic point in your program is a big help. The statement should print the values of variables to show whether the results are correct at that point. These statements also show which parts of the program have been executed. The use of debugging statements can be very helpful in identifying and correcting any errors.

Finishing Touches

Another way to debug your program is to debug the object code. This requires more knowledge of how the computer works. It also requires a knowledge of hexadecimal numbers, described in Appendix B, and of ASCII code, described in Appendix C. Knowledge of assembly language helps, too. Since debugging the object code can be time-consuming, especially if you are learning to do it as you go along, you should first try to find the problem by using debugging statements in your program. If that fails, then debug the object code.

A utility supplied with the Lattice C Compiler and an option of LC1 help you to get started. The Object Module Disassembler (OMD) is a utility that shows you the machine code produced by the compiler. If you run LC1 using the $-d$ option, the listing from OMD shows you the machine code results from each statement of your program.

Once you have decided to debug the object code, decide which object module needs to be debugged. Then recompile that module using a command like this:

LC1 B:PROG $-d$

The intermediate code written by LC1 using the $-d$ option contains "hooks" that associate each source statement with the resulting code. Run LC2 in the usual way:

LC2 B:PROG

LC2 passes the "hooks" from LC1 along to the object module it writes. Now you are ready to run OMD. Type:

OMD >B:PROG.LST B:PROG.OBJ B:PROG.C

Notice that, unlike the compiler and LINK, OMD does not supply the extensions; you must include them in the file specifications. On file B:PROG.LST, OMD lists the contents of object module B:PROG.OBJ interspersed with statements from source file B:PROG.C.

OMD contains four data areas for four categories of information it uses in processing an object module. Each area is large enough to allow OMD to process a typical object module. If your object module overflows one of these areas, OMD issues an error message that tells you which area is not large enough. In that case, use the appropriate option to increase the size of that data area. See the Lattice C manual for complete information about the Object Module Disassembler options.

Chapter 11

OMD *disassembles* the object (machine) code in an object module. That is, it arranges the code into the machine instructions, and supplies the mnemonic operation code for each instruction. It also lists the data of your program.

Figure 11-3 shows the OMD listing of a program that is used as the example program for debugging. Notice that the first section lists external definitions. In this case, the program consists of only the *main*( ) function; that is the only external definition. This section would also include definitions of any other functions in this module and of any external data items defined in this module. The number following *main* is a four-digit hexadecimal number. It is the offset of the start of function *main;* it is relative to the code segment. The letter that follows the offset is P for program. It would be D for a data item.

Next comes the program section of the listing, introduced by a label that gives the size of the section in bytes. If 15C does not look like a number to you, it is because the number is a hexadecimal number. If you need to learn about hexadecimal numbers, go to Appendix B. You will not be able to continue debugging the object code without a working knowledge of hexadecimal numbers. The only decimal numbers on this listing are the numbers in the source program statements interspersed with the machine code.

The listing is arranged in four columns. The first column contains the offset of the first instruction. The second column contains the machine code of the instruction. This is the hexadecimal representation of the ones and zeros that tell the microprocessor what to do. The third column contains the instruction *mnemonic*, the symbolic name of the instruction. The fourth column contains the *operands* of the instruction. The operands tell the microprocessor where the data for the operation is.

The first seven lines of the program section manage the stack. In the discussion of the scope of variables in Chapter 5, I mentioned that *automatic* type variables go on the stack. So do the arguments for a function. The machine instructions on these first seven lines store the current stack position and test the remaining portion of the stack to be sure the stack does not overflow while this function executes. The compiler puts

Finishing Touches

these instructions at the beginning of every function. They do not directly relate to any statement in your program; they are *overhead*.

Next, OMD has inserted seven source program lines. None of the first six lines produces executable code; the machine instruction listing resumes after the seventh line, displaying the instructions that correspond to the statement on that line.

The statement on the seventh line calls function **printf( )** to display a string constant supplied as the control string. The function call has one argument: the control string. The machine language moves the address of the control string (in the data section) to register AX, and pushes that address onto the stack. Then it calls the function.

In a similar manner, the rest of the instructions in the program section correspond to the source statements. Following the program section is the data section. It contains the static data for the object module. All of the control strings for the **printf( )** and **scanf( )** functions are in the data section, along with data items for other functions.

The data section shows the offset of the first byte on each line in the first column. To the right are 16 pairs of hexadecimal digits. Each pair represents the ones and zeros in a byte of memory. To the right of the hexadecimal representation is the character representation of the contents of the same 16 bytes. Notice that a period can represent either a period (.) or the contents of a byte that contains a nonprinting character.

Do not attempt to master the OMD listing at this point. Instead, refer to it to identify the type of instruction at a certain offset or the character in a byte at another offset. As you locate specific information you need for debugging, you will learn to use the listing effectively. You don't have to understand everything on the listing to be able to use it.

If you did not specify a link map when you linked your program, link your program again to get a link map. The subsection on the link map in this chapter tells you how.

Chapter 11

Figure 11-3. OMD Sample Listing

LATTICE C OBJECT MODULE DISASSEMBLER V1.01
8086/8088 Instruction Set
EXTERNAL DEFINITIONS
    MAIN 0000-P
PROGRAM SECTION: 15C BYTES

```
0000    55                      PUSH    BP
0001    83EC40                  SUB     SP,40
0004    7206                    JB      000C
0006    3B26 0000-X             CMP     SP,[_BASE]
000A    7703                    JA      000F
000C    E9 0000-X               JMPL    XCOVF
000F    8BEC                    MOV     BP,SP
```
#include <math.h>
#include <limits.h>
main ( ) /* Compute mortgage payments */
{
double pr, factor;
double amt, in, n;
printf ("Amount of mortgage: $");
```
0011    B8 0000-D               MOV     AX,D.0000
0014    50                      PUSH    AX
0015    E8 0000-X               CALL    PRINTF
0018    8BE5                    MOV     SP,BP
```
scanf ("%lf",&pr);
```
001A    8D4618                  LEA     AX,[BP+18]
001D    50                      PUSH    AX
001E    B8 1600-D               MOV     AX,D.0016
0021    50                      PUSH    AX
0022    E8 0000-X               CALL    SCANF
0025    8BE5                    MOV     SP,BP
```
printf (" \nInterest — Percent per year: ");
```
0027    B8 1A00-D               MOV     AX,D.001A
002A    50                      PUSH    AX
002B    E8 0000-X               CALL    PRINTF
002E    8BE5                    MOV     SP,BP
```
scanf ("%lf",&in);
```
0030    8D4630                  LEA     AX,[BP+30]
0033    50                      PUSH    AX
0034    B8 1600-D               MOV     AX,D.0016
0037    50                      PUSH    AX
0038    E8 0000-X               CALL    SCANF
003B    8BE5                    MOV     SP,BP
```
in = in/100.0;

003D	8B4636	MOV	AX,[BP+36]
0040	8B5E34	MOV	BX,[BP+34]
0043	8B4E32	MOV	CX,[BP+32]
0046	8B5630	MOV	DX,[BP+30]
0049	BE 6800-D	MOV	SI,D.0068
004C	56	PUSH	SI
004D	E8 0000-X	CALL	CXD55

printf (" \nNumber of monthly payments: ");

0050	894636	MOV	[BP+36],AX
0053	895E34	MOV	[BP+34],BX
0056	894E32	MOV	[BP+32],CX
0059	895630	MOV	[BP+30],DX
005C	B8 3900-D	MOV	AX,D.0039
005F	50	PUSH	AX
0060	E8 0000-X	CALL	PRINTF
0063	8BE5	MOV	SP,BP

scanf ("%lf",&n);

0065	8D4638	LEA	AX,[BP+38]
0068	50	PUSH	AX
0069	B8 1600-D	MOV	AX,D.0016
006C	50	PUSH	AX
006D	E8 0000-X	CALL	SCANF
0070	8BE5	MOV	SP,BP

factor = 1.0 + in/12.0;

0072	8B4636	MOV	AX,[BP+36]
0075	8B5E34	MOV	BX,[BP+34]
0078	8B4E32	MOV	CX,[BP+32]
007B	8B5630	MOV	DX,[BP+30]
007E	BE 7000-D	MOV	SI,D.0070
0081	56	PUSH	SI
0082	E8 0000-X	CALL	CXD55
0085	BE 7800-D	MOV	SI,D.0078
0088	56	PUSH	SI
0089	E8 0000-X	CALL	CXA55

amt = (pr*in/12.0) / (1 − exp(−n * log(factor)));

008C	894626	MOV	[BP+26],AX
008F	895E24	MOV	[BP+24],BX
0092	894E22	MOV	[BP+22],CX
0095	895620	MOV	[BP+20],DX
0098	8B461E	MOV	AX,[BP+1E]
009B	8B5E1C	MOV	BX,[BP+1C]
009E	8B4E1A	MOV	CX,[BP+1A]
00A1	8B5618	MOV	DX,[BP+18]
00A4	8D7630	LEA	SI,[BP+30]
00A7	56	PUSH	SI
00A8	E8 0000-X	CALL	CXM55

Chapter 11

00AB	BE 7000-D	MOV	SI,D.0070
00AE	56	PUSH	SI
00AF	E8 0000-X	CALL	CXD55
00B2	894606	MOV	[BP+06],AX
00B5	895E04	MOV	[BP+04],BX
00B8	894E02	MOV	[BP+02],CX
00BB	895600	MOV	[BP+00],DX
00BE	8B463E	MOV	AX,[BP+3E]
00C1	8B5E3C	MOV	BX,[BP+3C]
00C4	8B4E3A	MOV	CX,[BP+3A]
00C7	8B5638	MOV	DX,[BP+38]
00CA	E8 0000-X	CALL	CXN5
00CD	89460E	MOV	[BP+0E],AX
00D0	895E0C	MOV	[BP+0C],BX
00D3	894E0A	MOV	[BP+0A],CX
00D6	895608	MOV	[BP+08],DX
00D9	8B4626	MOV	AX,[BP+26]
00DC	8B5E24	MOV	BX,[BP+24]
00DF	8B4E22	MOV	CX,[BP+22]
00E2	8B5620	MOV	DX,[BP+20]
00E5	50	PUSH	AX
00E6	53	PUSH	BX
00E7	51	PUSH	CX
00E8	52	PUSH	DX
00E9	E8 0000-X	CALL	LOG
00EC	8BE5	MOV	SP,BP
00EE	8D7608	LEA	SI,[BP+08]
00F1	56	PUSH	SI
00F2	E8 0000-X	CALL	CXM55
00F5	50	PUSH	AX
00F6	53	PUSH	BX
00F7	51	PUSH	CX
00F8	52	PUSH	DX
00F9	E8 0000-X	CALL	EXP
00FC	8BE5	MOV	SP,BP
00FE	894616	MOV	[BP+16],AX
0101	895E14	MOV	[BP+14],BX
0104	894E12	MOV	[BP+12],CX
0107	895610	MOV	[BP+10],DX
010A	BE 7800-D	MOV	SI,D.0078
010D	8B4406	MOV	AX,[SI+06]
0110	8B5C04	MOV	BX,[SI+04]
0113	8B4C02	MOV	CX,[SI+02]
0116	8B14	MOV	DX,[SI]
0118	8D7610	LEA	SI,[BP+10]
011B	56	PUSH	SI

Finishing Touches

```
011C    E8 0000-X            CALL   CXS55
011F    89460E               MOV    [BP+0E],AX
0122    895E0C               MOV    [BP+0C],BX
0125    894E0A               MOV    [BP+0A],CX
0128    895608               MOV    [BP+08],DX
012B    8B4606               MOV    AX,[BP+06]
012E    8B5E04               MOV    BX,[BP+04]
0131    8B4E02               MOV    CX,[BP+02]
0134    8B5600               MOV    DX,[BP+00]
0137    8D7608               LEA    SI,[BP+08]
013A    56                   PUSH   SI
013B    E8 0000-X            CALL   CXD55
printf (" \nPayment: $%.2lf",amt);
013E    50                   PUSH   AX
013F    53                   PUSH   BX
0140    51                   PUSH   CX
0141    52                   PUSH   DX
0142    89462E               MOV    [BP+2E],AX
0145    895E2C               MOV    [BP+2C],BX
0148    894E2A               MOV    [BP+2A],CX
014B    895628               MOV    [BP+28],DX
014E    B8 5700-D            MOV    AX,D.0057
0151    50                   PUSH   AX
0152    E8 0000-X            CALL   PRINTF
0155    8BE5                 MOV    SP,BP
} **END OF SOURCE FILE
0157    83C440               ADD    SP,40
015A    5D                   POP    BP
015B    C3                   RET
```

DATA SECTION: 80 BYTES
```
0000  41 6D 6F 75 6E 74 20 6F 66 20 6D 6F 72 74 67 61   Amount of mortga
0010  67 65 3A 20 24 00 25 6C 66 00 0A 49 6E 74 65 72   ge: $.%lf..Inter
0020  65 73 74 20 2D 20 50 65 72 63 65 6E 74 20 70 65   est — Percent pe
0030  72 20 79 65 61 72 3A 20 00 0A 4E 75 6D 62 65 72   r year: ..Number
0040  20 6F 66 20 6D 6F 6E 74 68 6C 79 20 70 61 79 6D    of monthly paym
0050  65 6E 74 73 3A 20 00 0A 50 61 79 6D 65 6E 74 3A   ents: ..Payment:
0060  20 24 25 2E 32 6C 66 00 00 00 00 00 00 00 59 40    $%.2lf.......Y@
0070  00 00 00 00 00 00 28 40 00 00 00 00 00 00 F0 3F   ......(@.....p?
```

181

Chapter 11

Using DEBUG

With your OMD listing and link map in hand, you are ready to use DEBUG. DEBUG is a machine language debugging program supplied with MS-DOS. You can read an executable module, look at the machine instructions and data it contains, and run the program under control of DEBUG. With DEBUG, you can execute the machine instructions one at a time and see what each instruction does. Or you can execute a function of the program and see that it does what it should and returns the proper value. To run DEBUG, type:

DEBUG B:PROG.EXE

If your program uses command line argument(s), type these argument(s) after the .EXE filename. When you press RETURN, DEBUG loads your program and displays a prompt character, waiting for a command.

The linking operation has changed the offsets you see on your OMD listing, and the loading operation has changed the segment addresses you see on your link map. But that's no big deal when you understand what happened and why. (See Appendix D for more information about segments and addressing.) Remember, you linked two object modules: CS and B:PROG. Because CS is first (and it *must* be first), the instructions in CS were placed ahead of those for B:PROG in the code segment when LINKed. So the offset for the first instruction of your object module is the offset shown for MAIN on the link map: 238 (see Figure 11-1). The actual offset you will use with DEBUG is the *hexadecimal* sum of the offset on the OMD listing and 238. If hexadecimal addition doesn't come naturally to you, don't worry. The HEX command of DEBUG will do it for you.

When the loader (part of MS-DOS used by DEBUG) loaded your executable module into memory, it put the module wherever it found space for it, setting segment addresses accordingly. So the segment addresses shown on the link map do not apply. This is not a problem because the loader, DEBUG, and the CS program take care of loading the proper values in the segment registers, and you should use the segment registers to address instructions and data items. Besides, DEBUG shows you the segment register contents.

Now that DEBUG has loaded your program, you can start debugging. Type

G249

Finishing Touches

and press RETURN. The G command causes DEBUG to execute the CS program and the first set of "overhead" instructions. When DEBUG finishes executing those instructions it displays:

```
AX=068E BX=0080 CX=020C DX=46B0 SP=137C BP=137C SI=0572 DI=0000
DS=0A57 ES=0A57 SS=0A57 CS=054A IP=0249   NV UP EI PL NZ NA PE NC
054A:0249 B8D000         MOV     AX,00D0
```

This display shows the complete state of the computer after executing the instruction preceding the one at offset 249. The top line shows the contents of the eight general-purpose registers. The left half of the second line shows the contents of the four segment registers. To the right of the segment registers is the Instruction Pointer (IP) register. It contains the offset of the next instruction to be executed: 0249. The pairs of letters to the right of the IP register indicate the states of the status flags, as follows:

NV Overflow Flag is 0; no overflow.
UP Direction Flag is 0; increment registers.
EI Interrupt Flag is 1; interrupts enabled.
PL Sign Flag is 0; result was positive (plus).
NZ Zero Flag is 0; result was not zero.
NA Auxiliary Carry Flag is 0; no auxiliary carry.
PE Parity Flag is 1; even parity.
NC Carry Flag is 0; no carry.

The third line is very similar to the line for offset 11 on the OMD listing (Figure 11-3). This line shows the next instruction to be executed. The segment address and offset, separated by a colon, are at the left end of the line. The segment address is 054A, determined by the point at which the loader loaded the program. If you are using a different version of MS-DOS, the segment addresses in your display are different from mine. This same value is in segment register CS, the segment register for the code segment. The offset is 0249, because the G command told DEBUG to execute the program up to that offset. The IP register contains the same offset.

Next comes the machine instruction. The offset portion of the machine instruction in the OMD listing is zero followed by −D. This means that the offset is determined by the linking process and is not available to OMD. On the DEBUG display, the offset is D000.

To the right of the machine instruction is the mnemonic for the instruction and its operands. These items are the same

183

Chapter 11

as those on the listing except that the offset has been supplied. Notice that the digits of the offset are arranged differently here. This is because the microprocessor reverses the order of the bytes of all numeric data in memory. The machine instruction has the offset as D000, the order in which the bytes are stored in memory. The operand representation shows the offset as 00D0, the actual offset value. You can prove this by typing:

DDS:00D0

This command tells DEBUG to display the contents of 512 bytes of memory starting at offset 00D0 relative to segment register DS. When you press RETURN, DEBUG displays the contents of memory, both in hexadecimal and character representations. The display is very similar to the data section of the OMD listing (Figure 11-3).

Now press the U key and press RETURN. This causes DEBUG to display the following (possibly with a different segment address):

```
054A:0249   B8D000      MOV    AX,00D0
054A:024C   50          PUSH   AX
054A:024D   E8EE02      CALL   053E
054A:0250   8BE5        MOV    SP,BP
054A:0252   8D4618      LEA    AX,[BP+18]
054A:0255   50          PUSH   AX
054A:0256   B8E600      MOV    AX,00E6
054A:0259   50          PUSH   AX
054A:025A   E86B01      CALL   03C8
054A:025D   8BE5        MOV    SP,BP
054A:025F   B8EA00      MOV    AX,00EA
054A:0262   50          PUSH   AX
054A:0263   E8D802      CALL   053E
054A:0266   8BE5        MOV    SP,BP
054A:0268   8D4630      LEA    AX,[BP+30]
```

This display shows the next 15 instructions, in the same format as the bottom line of the display shown above. Compare it to the program section of the OMD listing. The instructions are the same; operands that were not available to OMD have been inserted.

Now type T and press RETURN. This causes DEBUG to execute the MOV command at offset 249, and again display the status of the computer. Notice that the contents of register AX is now 00D0 and the contents of register IP is now 024C.

184

Finishing Touches

The instruction at 054A:024C is now displayed on the bottom line. Otherwise, the status is unchanged. The computer moved 00D0 into register AX as it was supposed to.

Type the T command again to execute the PUSH instruction. The SP register, which indicates the top of the stack, now contains 137A, indicating that a two-byte value was pushed onto the stack. The IP register contains 024D, and the displayed instruction is a CALL instruction.

If you continued to type in T commands, DEBUG would continue to execute instructions one by one. They would be the instructions of function **printf( )** (according to the OMD listing), which doesn't need to be debugged. Besides, you have no listing of **printf( )** to follow; you would lose track of what was going on. So, instead of walking through **printf( )**, look at the display provided by the U command to see the offset of the first instruction after the CALL instruction. The offset is 250; type this command:

G250

When you press RETURN, DEBUG executes all instructions in function **printf( )**, displaying the specified string:

Amount of mortgage: $

DEBUG also displays the status of the computer after executing the function. Notice that the contents of all registers except the SP, BP, and DI registers and the segment registers have changed. Two of the flags have changed. The new values are not important. From the displayed string you can tell that the function did what it was supposed to do. The IP register now contains 0250, the address of the next instruction.

The MS-DOS manual contains descriptions of these DEBUG commands and the other commands DEBUG provides. This introduction to DEBUG gives you an idea of how you can use it to check out your program at the machine instruction level. The more you use it, the easier it will be for you. But it is still not the best way to debug a program; it is tedious and time-consuming. Just use it when nothing else will do the job.

As you use DEBUG, sooner or later you will lose control of the program you are debugging, and you may think your computer is broken. The screen may be blank, or it may contain interesting characters scrolling rapidly upward, beeping now and then as they fly by. Try holding down the CTRL key and pressing the C key, which gets you out of a well-behaved

Chapter 11

program. If it works, type Q to get out of DEBUG, and run DEBUG again to continue debugging. If it doesn't work (and it won't if your program is truly out of hand), press CTRL, ALT, and DEL all together. That should cause the computer to perform its self-tests and reload MS-DOS (remember, you'll lose what's in memory by pressing CTRL, ALT, and DEL). If it does, run DEBUG again to continue debugging. As a last resort, turn the power off, then back on after 15 seconds. The computer should start over, testing itself and loading MS-DOS.

This traumatic experience may make you swear off computers for life, thinking you have broken something and that your computer will never be the same. What has actually happened is that an error in the program or in your debugging technique has got the program into an endless loop or into an area of data which it is trying to execute as instructions. Just regain control of your computer as described in the preceding paragraph, and continue debugging. Until the error is found and corrected, though, the same thing will happen again. Carefully examine the program to attempt to identify the error. Or, as you continue to debug, try to isolate the area of the program in which you lose control, and look very closely at the statements in that portion of your program.

One thing more. DEBUG's G command is a very useful command, but one that can get you into trouble. If the offset you supply with the G command is not the offset of the first byte of an instruction, processing continues to the end of the program or to a point where you lose control of the computer. Similarly, if the offset you type with the G command is that of an instruction that the program does not execute (because the program takes a different branch, for example), the same thing happens. However, nothing really breaks. Just reload your program and try again.

Appendices

Appendix A
C Language Summary

Keywords

auto	break	case	char
continue	default	do	double
else	entry	extern	float
for	goto	if	int
long	register	return	short
sizeof	static	struct	switch
typedef	union	unsigned	while

Data Types

Type	Bytes (8086/8088)
char	1
int	2
short	2
unsigned	2
long	4
float	4
double	8
struct	n/a
union	n/a

Storage Class Specifiers

auto	extern
register	static

Appendix A

Operators
(in order of priority)

```
()      []      ->      .
!       ~       ++      --      -       (type)  *       &       sizeof
*       /       %
+       -
<<      >>
<       <=      >       >=
==      !=
&
^
|
&&
||
?:      (conditional expression)
=       +=      -=      *=      /=      %=      >>=     <<=     &=      ^=      |=
,       (in for statement)
```

Statements

if (*expression*)
else (*expression*)
while (*expression*)
do
while (*expression*) ;
for (*expression* ; *expression* ; *expression*)
switch (*expression*) {
    case *constant-expression* :
    default :
    }
break ;
continue ;
return (*expression*)
goto *label*

Compiler Control Lines

#define   #else
#endif   #if
#ifdef   #ifndef
#include   #undef

C Language Summary

Conversion Specifications for printf( ) and scanf( )

Specification	Type of Conversion
%d	Decimal
%o	Octal
%x	Hexadecimal
%u	Unsigned integer
%f	Floating point
%e	Exponential format
%s	Character string
%c	Single character

For printf( ) only:

%g	Either %e or %f

For scanf( ) only:

%h	Short integer

Appendix B
Hexadecimal Numbers

Don't let hexadecimal numbers be a problem for you. Most of the numbers you see on program listings are hexadecimal numbers, not decimal numbers. All of the numbers displayed by the DEBUG utility are hexadecimal numbers. If you're going to use this valuable information, you'll have to have a working knowledge of hexadecimal numbers. They're not difficult if you avoid getting bogged down in number theory and concentrate on learning how to use them.

Theory

Hexadecimal numbers are numbers that use the *base*, or *radix*, of 16 instead of 10, the base of the familiar decimal numbers. Just as the positions of decimal digits (1's, 10's, 100's, and so forth) represent powers of 10, the positions of hexadecimal digits represent powers of 16 (1's, 16's, 256's,...).

Decimal digits represent powers of 10, so there are ten decimal digits: 0, 1, 2, 3, 4, 5, 6, 7, 8, and 9. Hexadecimal digits represent powers of 16; thus, 16 hexadecimal digits: 0, 1, 2, 3, 4, 5, 6, 7, 8, 9, A, B, C, D, E, and F. The values of the letters in decimal are 10 for A, 11 for B, 12 for C, 13 for D, 14 for E, and 15 for F. Why not use the numbers then? Because each of these numbers consists of two decimal digits that represent a single hexadecimal digit. The hexadecimal number system arbitrarily uses these letters as symbols for numeric digits.

This is one of the biggest problems people have with hexadecimal numbers. All our lives we have known that the ABCs are *letters*. We just can't have much confidence in anyone who says that A, B, C, D, E, and F are *numbers*. Why, that sort of person might try to tell us anything. If you can just get

Appendix B

over the mental block that these letters are digits with numerical values, you'll be well on your way to a working knowledge of hexadecimal.

Working Knowledge

So much for the theory. What you need is to be able to use the information shown in hexadecimal notation. The most important thing to remember is that hexadecimal numbers have different values: hexadecimal 10 is not 10, but decimal 16. Furthermore, hexadecimal 5 plus hexadecimal 6 is not hexadecimal 11, but hexadecimal B. Don't try to remember the new values; your computer can do the figuring for you. Just don't forget that hexadecimal numbers have different values, and if you have to add, decimal addition doesn't produce the correct results.

Hexadecimal numbers are used with computers because they are a convenient way of expressing the binary numbers the computer actually uses. Each hexadecimal digit represents four binary digits (bits); see Table B-1. If you had a binary address like this, it would be hard to copy accurately:

1010010111000010

You can make four groups of four bits each from the number:

1010 0101 1100 0010

Now, using Table B-1, find the hexadecimal digit that corresponds to each group of bits, and you have an address that is almost as easy to work with as a decimal number:

A5C2

Hexadecimal Arithmetic

You seldom need to know the decimal equivalent of a hexadecimal address, but you may have to add or subtract hexadecimal addresses. Just use DEBUG. Type:

DEBUG

When DEBUG is ready for a command, it displays its prompt. Type in the H command followed by two hexadecimal numbers:

HA5C2 0050

194

Hexadecimal Numbers

DEBUG displays the sum and the difference:

A612 A572

The H (for hexadecimal) command of DEBUG is very handy to help you with hexadecimal arithmetic. You don't need to type four digits if a number has only two significant digits (0050, for example). Just type the significant digits.

However, the result is always shown as four digits, even when an overflow to the fifth digit occurs. For example,

H8346 8345

068B 0001

The actual sum is hexadecimal 1068B, but the H command doesn't display the leading 1. Another surprise occurs when the difference is negative. It is displayed in *twos-complement* form:

H6472 A24B

06BD C227

The difference is C227. The negative difference is the twos complement of this value. To find the twos-complement value, start with its absolute value of C227. Expressed as a binary number, the absolute value is:

1100001000100111

To obtain the twos complement of a binary number, change all zeros to ones and all ones to zeros; then add 1:

0011110111011000
0000000000000001
0011110111011001

Now translate this to hexadecimal by separating the 16 bits into four groups of four bits each:

0011 1101 1101 1001

Referring to Table B-1, this is equal to 3DD9. This is the result of subtracting A24B from 6472; it's a negative number.

Hexadecimal Conversions

You often need to convert decimal data to hexadecimal numbers, and hexadecimal results to decimal values. You can use the *convert* program example shown in Chapter 4, or you can modify it by using the example functions from Chapter 5.

195

Appendix B

Compile and link the program as described in Chapter 11, storing the executable module as CONVERT.EXE. Then type:

CONVERT 654

When you press RETURN, CONVERT displays:

654 converts to 0x28E

This shows you the hexadecimal equivalent of a decimal number. It works the other way, too:

CONVERT 0x24B3

0x24B3 converts to 9395

This time CONVERT provides the decimal equivalent of a hexadecimal number.

The maximum decimal number that can be converted correctly is 65,535. The maximum hexadecimal number that can be converted correctly is 0xFFFF. The offsets and segment addresses you use in debugging are within these limits.

Bit-Picking

Chapter 5 describes a structure that you can use to divide the bits of an integer into fields that you can address using identifiers. Sometimes you need to know the value in a field, and all you have is the hexadecimal value of the integer. As an example, this structure divides an integer into fields that represent a garden club member's status and interests:

```
struct {
   unsigned voting   : 1;
   unsigned assoc    : 1;
   unsigned life     : 1;
   unsigned current  : 1;
   unsigned flowers  : 1;
   unsigned vegs     : 1;
   unsigned lawns    : 1;
   unsigned trees    : 1;
   unsigned cacti    : 1;
   unsigned herbs    : 1;
} status;
```

DEBUG tells us the integer contains hexadecimal 9AC0. To translate that value into the fields of the structure, first substitute the binary values for the hexadecimal digits:

1001101011000000

Hexadecimal Numbers

Computers that run MS-DOS define the fields from left to right. So match the bits with the fields from left to right: *status.voting* has a value of 1 and *status.assoc* is 0; *status.current*, *status.flowers*, *status.lawns*, *status.cacti*, and *status.herbs* also are set to 1. The other fields are set to 0. So this member is a voting member whose dues are current. The member is interested in flowers, lawns, cacti, and herbs.

Table B-1. Hexadecimal Digits

Digit	Decimal Value	Binary Value
0	0	0000
1	1	0001
2	2	0010
3	3	0011
4	4	0100
5	5	0101
6	6	0110
7	7	0111
8	8	1000
9	9	1001
A	10	1010
B	11	1011
C	12	1100
D	13	1101
E	14	1110
F	15	1111

Appendix C
ASCII Code

The *American Standard Code for Information Interchange* (ASCII) has become the standard computer code, especially for microcomputers. The following table shows the codes in decimal and hexadecimal, along with the control characters, letters, numerals, and special characters they represent.

ASCII Code Table

Character	Dec	Hex	Character	Dec	Hex
NUL	0	0	FS	28	1C
SOH	1	1	GS	29	1D
STX	2	2	RS	30	1E
ETX	3	3	US	31	1F
EOT	4	4	SP	32	20
ENQ	5	5	!	33	21
ACK	6	6	"	34	22
BEL	7	7	#	35	23
BS	8	8	$	36	24
HT	9	9	%	37	25
LF	10	A	&	38	26
VT	11	B	'	39	27
FF	12	C	(	40	28
CR	13	D	)	41	29
SO	14	E	*	42	2A
SI	15	F	+	43	2B
DLE	16	10	,	44	2C
DC1	17	11	-	45	2D
DC2	18	12	.	46	2E
DC3	19	13	/	47	2F
DC4	20	14	0	48	30
NAK	21	15	1	49	31
SYN	22	16	2	50	32
ETB	23	17	3	51	33
CAN	24	18	4	52	34
EM	25	19	5	53	35
SUB	26	1A	6	54	36
ESC	27	1B	7	55	37

Appendix C

Character	Dec	Hex	Character	Dec	Hex
8	56	38	\	92	5C
9	57	39	]	93	5D
:	58	3A	^	94	5E
;	59	3B	_	95	5F
<	60	3C	'	96	60
=	61	3D	a	97	61
>	62	3E	b	98	62
?	63	3F	c	99	63
@	64	40	d	100	64
A	65	41	e	101	65
B	66	42	f	102	66
C	67	43	g	103	67
D	68	44	h	104	68
E	69	45	i	105	69
F	70	46	j	106	6A
G	71	47	k	107	6B
H	72	48	l	108	6C
I	73	49	m	109	6D
J	74	4A	n	110	6E
K	75	4B	o	111	6F
L	76	4C	p	112	70
M	77	4D	q	113	71
N	78	4E	r	114	72
O	79	4F	s	115	73
P	80	50	t	116	74
Q	81	51	u	117	75
R	82	52	v	118	76
S	83	53	w	119	77
T	84	54	x	120	78
U	85	55	y	121	79
V	86	56	z	122	7A
W	87	57	{	123	7B
X	88	58			124	7C
Y	89	59	}	125	7D
Z	90	5A	~	126	7E
[	91	5B	DEL	127	7F

Appendix D
Microprocessor Addressing

The debugging information in Chapter 11 refers to segment addresses and offsets. While you don't need to know a great deal about the internal workings of the microprocessor in your computer, the development of an actual memory address from a segment address is not intuitively obvious. In case you don't know about segments, this appendix describes memory addressing in greater detail.

This addressing information applies directly to the IBM PC and compatibles. Specifically, it applies to computers that use the 8086, 8088, 80186, and 80188 microprocessors. Additional information applicable to the IBM AT and its compatibles, which use the 80286 microprocessor, is included at the end of the appendix.

Memory Addressing
The address space of the microprocessor consists of one megabyte (1M) of storage. I haven't heard of a personal computer that has that much memory, but the microprocessor could address any one of those bytes if you had that much memory. The format of machine instructions provides 16 bits for address information. These 16 bits can address only 65,536 (64K) bytes. It takes a 20-bit address to provide 1M addresses.

The microprocessor solves this problem by using a *segment address* (16 bits) and an *offset* (16 bits). It combines these two values to get the necessary 20-bit address. It adds the offset portion to the 20-bit value resulting from multiplying the segment address by 16. For example, if the segment address is 2A46 and the offset is 0742, the actual address is 2ABA2:

Segment address * 16	2A460
Offset	0742
Actual Address	2ABA2

201

Appendix D

Segment Registers

The microprocessor has four segment registers that contain four segment addresses:

DS register   Data segment
CS register   Code segment
SS register   Stack segment
ES register   Extra segment

    The machine instructions that address data in memory contain an offset, either in the instruction or in a register. The offset is combined with the segment address in register DS to get the actual address of the data. The actual address of an instruction is derived from a segment address in the CS register combined with the offset in the IP register. Similarly, the actual address of the word at the top of the stack is derived from the segment address in the SS register and the offset in the SP register. The actual destination address for a string instruction is derived from the segment address in the ES register and the offset in the DI register.

    Thus, a given value in register CS with an offset in the IP register can address 64K different bytes (one for each possible offset value). Changing the contents of the segment register makes a different set (possibly an overlapping set) of 64K bytes accessible. The same flexibility applies to addresses derived from the other three segment registers. The segment and offset addressing technique used in these microprocessors is very efficient and flexible.

    Many programs use a format that places the same segment address in all four segment registers. As mentioned in Chapter 11, a C program that uses the S or P memory model places one value in the CS register and another value in the CS, SS, and ES registers. C programs that use the D or L model run with different values in each segment register.

    A segment can begin at any address that is an even multiple of 16. That is, any of the 65,536 values that you can put in a segment register is valid. It's most convenient to start a segment at a zero offset, making it possible for the segment to contain the full 64K bytes.

Advanced Microcomputers

The IBM AT, the TI Business-Pro, and their compatibles use the same segment registers and offsets to derive addresses.

Microprocessor Addressing

The microprocessor in these computers (80286) has two addressing modes: compatible (real) and protected. In the compatible mode, the segment registers contain the most significant portions of actual memory addresses, just as they do in the earlier microprocessors. The actual addresses are developed in the same way.

In the protected mode the segment registers contain *virtual* memory segment addresses. The address is called a virtual address because the segment may not *actually* be in memory at any particular time. The memory management portion of the microprocessor translates the virtual address into an actual address, reading the memory contents from the disk when necessary. This technique makes a great many more bytes of memory available to the microprocessor. Not only that, but the memory management circuitry uses a *protection* technique to prevent programs from accessing each other's memory areas.

Your application program, however, does not concern itself with memory management. The 16-bit segment address and the 16-bit offset still combine to provide the address of an actual memory location. The linking process and the loading operation provide the proper offsets in the instructions and the proper contents for the segment registers. The loading operation sets the necessary variables to properly relate the segment register values to the actual storage areas of memory. This enables memory management circuitry in the microprocessor to do all the work. Your program just uses segments and offsets, as in the earlier microprocessors.

The designers of the 80286 microprocessor have done a good job. They have added memory management capabilities to the microprocessor that provide a whole new order of memory capacity. Yet they have done it without making existing software obsolete. Existing software runs without modification (and without utilizing the full capabilities of the microprocessor). New software runs, too, exploiting the additional capabilities of the 80286.

Index

! (NOT) operator 22, 95, 96
!= (not equal) operator 15, 38
#define compiler control line 87, 118, 141, 147, 148, 152, 154
#else compiler control line 153
#endif compiler control line 152
#if compiler control line 152
#ifdef compiler control line 153
#ifndef compiler control line 153
#include compiler control line 141, 146, 147
#undef compiler control line 151, 152
% (conversion specification) 103
% (modulo) operator 15, 103
& (address) operator 51, 80, 81
& (bit-by-bit AND) operator 22, 95
&& (AND) operator 22, 94
* (indirect) operator 81, 82, 87
++ (increment) operator 23 99, 101, 150
−− (decrement) operator 23, 101, 150
-> (indirect membership) operator 88
-d compiler option 175
-i compiler option 164
-m compiler option 165
-o compiler option 165
. (membership) operator 88
/ (division) operator 15
/M linking option 169
<< (left shift) operator 22, 98
== (equal) operator 15, 93
>> (right shift) operator 22, 98
\n (newline) character 49, 124, 129, 130, 142
\0 (null) character 13, 63, 78, 129, 142
^ (bit-by-bit exclusive OR) operator 22, 96
| (bit-by-bit OR) operator 22, 96
|| (OR) operator 22, 94
~ (bit-by-bit NOT) operator 22, 95
abs( ) function 151
address, segment 69, 169, 182, 196, 201
address arithmetic 28
address space 201
ambiguous operators 102
American Standard Code for Information Interchange (ASCII) 199
ANSI standard 9
append file 131
argument 45, 53
   call by reference 80

call by value 80
   formal 72, 81
arithmetic
   address 28
   hexadecimal 194
   pointer 28, 85
arithmetic expression 15
arithmetic operator 93
arithmetic progression 20
array 22, 27, 77, 105, 116
   character 78
   data structure 65, 79
   initialization 87
   notation 85
   pointer 83–85, 86, 87
   single-dimensioned 78
   three-dimensioned 77
   two-dimensioned 78
ASCII code 199
assignment expression 104
assignment operator 23, 104
assignment statement 15, 33, 81
association, operator 102
atob( ) example function 55
atou( ) example function 57
automatic type conversion 39
auto storage class 72, 176
base 193
BASIC string array 63
big( ) example function 83
   alternative 84
binary number 194
block 11, 24, 36, 38
break statement 21, 116
bubble sort 86
byte 73, 137
call
   function 150
   macro 150
call by reference argument 80
call by value argument 80
case prefix 21
cast operator 48, 99
change( ) example function 52
character
   character array 78
   character constant 13
   characteristics 9
   characters, control 139
char type 48, 63, 126
      \n (newline) 49, 124, 129, 130, 142

\0 (null) 13, 63, 78, 129, 142
CTRL-Z 167
  end-of-file 167
checkbook example program 40
class, storage 68, 189
clear( ) example function 49
CLOSE BASIC statement 132
close error 133
code segment 164, 202
comment 46
compatible mode 203
compiled language 3
compiler
  phase 1 162, 164
  phase 2 162, 165
compiler control line, conditional 152
compiler control lines 40, 50, 130, 145, 190
  #define 87, 118, 141, 147, 148, 152, 154
  #else 153
  #endif 152
  #if 152
  #ifdef 153
  #ifndef 153
  #include 141, 146, 147
  #undef 151, 152
compiler error messages 170
compiler options
  -d 175
  -i 164
  -m 165
  -o 165
compound statement 11, 36, 38
concepts 9
conditional compiler control line 152
conditional expression 19, 103
constant 12
  character 13
  string 13
  symbolic 50, 87, 199
continue statement 21, 117
control, loss of 185
control characters 139
control lines, compiler. *See* compiler control lines
control string 124, 128
conversion specification 103, 124, 125, 171, 191
convert numbers example program 53, 195
COPY command 166
copy word example 111
CS module 163
CS register 202
CTRL-Z character 167

data formatting 126
data segment 164, 202
data structure 25, 64, 132, 134
data structure array 65, 79
data structure initialization 64
DEBUG (MS-DOS program) 168, 182, 183
debug example program 155
debugging 154, 174
declarator 12, 17, 27, 33, 46, 61, 73, 81, 99, 133, 138, 146
default prefix 21
DEF FN BASIC statement 23
device name 138
dhconv( ) example function 55
  alternative 67
digit, hexadecimal 197
DIM BASIC statement 27, 77
directive, preprocessor 50, 145
disciplined programming 9, 12
display, DEBUG 183
display( ) example function 48
division, modulo 36
D memory model 165, 166, 202
double-precision type 62
double type 34, 62, 126
do while loop 21, 112
draw( ) example function 105
  alternative 113
DS register 202
EDLIN text editor 161
else if statement 20, 109
end-of-file character 167
EQV BASIC operator 97
error, close 133
error messages
  compiler 170
  linking 174
ES register 202
example functions
  atob( ) 55
  atou( ) 57
  big( ) 83
  change( ) 52
  clear( ) 49
  dhconv( ) 55
  display( ) 48
  draw( ) 105
  get( ) 137
  getts( ) 141
  hash( ) 118
  hdconv( ) 54
  item( ) 52
  kilometers( ) 47
  mid( ) 82
  put( ) 136

206

puthex( ) 67
sort( ) 87
studs( ) 46
sum( ) 51
taxcomp( ) 52
time( ) 81
example programs
  checkbook 40
  convert numbers 53, 195
  debug 155
  ring up 50
  special print 140
examples
  copy word 111
  menu 113
  print string 115
  random seed 111
  reverse string 111
  search 117
  square root 149
executable file 163, 166
executable program 4, 12
executable statement 46
expression
  arithmetic 15
  assignment 104
  conditional 19, 103
  logical 95
  relational 38
extern storage class 69, 70
extra segment 164, 202
fabs( ) function 152
fclose( ) function 133, 139
feof( ) function 132, 138
fgets( ) function 133
field 25, 65, 79, 95, 196
FIELD BASIC statement 134
file
  append 131
  executable 163, 166
  header 146, 150
  library 12, 166, 167
  MS-DOS sequential 133
  response 166
  stdio.h 130, 146, 151
  write 131
file identifier 130
float type 33, 62, 126
fopen( ) function 131, 134, 139
FOR BASIC statement 14, 37
for loop 14, 19, 37, 39, 49, 73, 99, 110
formal argument 72, 81
formatting data 126
fprintf( ) function 139
fputs( ) function 133, 139
fread( ) function 132, 138
fseek( ) function 136

function call 150
functions 10, 16, 35, 45
  abs( ) 151
  fabs( ) 152
  fclose( ) 133, 139
  feof( ) 132, 138
  fgets( ) 133
  fopen( ) 131, 134, 139
  fprintf( ) 139
  fputs( ) 133, 139
  fread( ) 132, 138
  fseek( ) 136
  fwrite( ) 132, 136, 137
  getch( ) 129
  getchar( ) 94
  getche( ) 40, 129
  gets( ) 28, 129, 135
  kbhit( ) 111
  log( ) 99
  main( ) 16, 17, 18, 23, 24, 50, 53, 100
  printf( ) 28, 40, 49, 103, 124, 125, 127, 135, 174, 177
  putc( ) 28
  putch( ) 49, 127
  puts( ) 127
  rand( ) 105
  scanf( ) 38, 40, 51, 127, 177
  srand( ) 106
  strcat( ) 142
  strcpy( ) 79
  strlen( ) 99, 142
functions, BASIC
  MID$ 82
  MKS$ 134
functions, input/output 58
functions, library 57
fwrite( ) function 132, 136, 137
geometric progression 20
GET BASIC statement 137
get( ) example function 137
getch( ) function 129
getchar( ) function 94
getche( ) function 40, 129
gets( ) function 28, 129, 135
getts( ) example function 141
GOTO BASIC statement 16, 21, 39, 109
goto statement 16, 39
hash code 118, 135
hash( ) example function 118
hdconv( ) example function 54
header file 146, 150
hexadecimal arithmetic 194
hexadecimal digit 197
hexadecimal number 168, 193
  theory 193
IBM AT microcomputer 202
identifier, file 130

207

if else statement 13, 35, 41, 54, 79, 93
IF-THEN-ELSE BASIC statement 13, 19, 20, 35, 103
IMP BASIC operator 97
initialization
  array 87
  data structure 64
INPUT BASIC statement 28, 127, 135
INPUT # BASIC statement 131
input device, standard 128
input/output 123
input/output functions 58
instruction, machine 4, 183, 201
integer variable 61
interpreted language 3
int type 61, 98, 126
item( ) example function 52
kbhit( ) function 111
key, sort 86
keywords, language 189
kilometers( ) example function 47
label 16, 39
language
  compiled 3
  interpreted 3
  keywords 189
LC1 162, 164
LC2 162, 165
LET BASIC statement 15
library file 12, 166, 167
library functions 57
library manager, PLIB86 168
linking 4, 35, 68, 151, 162, 165, 167, 203
linking error messages 174
linking option, /M 169
link map 168, 170, 177
L memory model 165, 166, 202
loading 203
log( ) function 99
logical expression 95
logical operation 94
long float type 62
long int type 61, 126, 137
loop
  do while 21, 112
  for 14, 19, 37, 39, 49, 73, 99, 110
  while 14, 17, 38, 41, 105
LPRINT BASIC statement 139
LSET BASIC statement 135
machine instruction 4, 183, 201
macro 148, 149
macro call 150
main( ) function 16, 17, 18, 23, 24, 50, 53, 100
maintenance, program 17, 147

management, memory 203
map, link 168, 170, 177
mask 66, 96
memory, virtual 203
memory management 203
memory models
  D 165, 166, 202
  L 165, 166, 202
  P 165, 166, 202
  S 164, 165, 169, 202
menu example 113
MID$ BASIC function 82
mid( ) example function 82
MKS$ BASIC function 134
mnemonic 176
mode
  compatible 203
  protected 203
  translated 131
mode string 131, 134
MOD operator 15
module CS, 163
modulo division 36
MS-DOS sequential file 133
name, device 138
NEXT BASIC statement 14, 37
notation
  array 85
  pointer 85
null record 137
null statement 112
number
  binary 194
  hexadecimal 168, 193
  octal 126
Object Module Disassembler (OMD) 175, 176, 178
object program 4
octal number 126
offset 69, 169, 177, 182, 183, 186, 196, 201
OMD. *See* Object Module Disassembler
OPEN BASIC statement 130, 133
operands 176
operation, logical 94
operator association 102
operator priority 101
operators 190
  ! (NOT) 22, 95, 96
  != (not equal) 15, 38
  % (modulo) 15, 103
  & (address) 51, 80, 81
  & (bit-by-bit AND) 22, 95
  && (AND) 22, 94
  * (indirect) 81, 82, 87
  ++ (increment) 23, 99, 101, 150

−− (decrement) 23, 101, 150
-> (indirect membership) 88
. (membership) 88
/ (division) 15
<< (left shift) 22, 98
== (equal) 15, 93
>> (right shift) 22, 98
^ (bit-by-bit exclusive OR) 22, 96
| (bit-by-bit OR) 22, 96
|| (OR) 22, 94
~ (bit-by-bit NOT) 22, 95
arithmetic 93
assignment 23, 104
cast 48, 99
MOD 15
relational 15
sizeof 98, 136, 148
operators, ambiguous 102
operators, BASIC
    EQV 97
    IMP 97
    XOR 127
OPTION BASE BASIC statement 27
output device, standard 124
PLIB86 library manager 168
P memory model 165, 166, 202
pointer 27, 51, 65, 80, 81, 82, 84, 101, 128
    array 83
pointer arithmetic 28, 85
pointer array 86, 87
pointer notation 85
postfix 23, 100
prefix 23, 100
    case 21
    default 21
preprocessor 145
preprocessor directive 50, 145
PRINT BASIC statement 28, 124, 127
PRINT # BASIC statement 132
printf( ) function 28, 40, 49, 103, 124, 125, 127, 135, 174, 177
print string example 115
PRINT USING BASIC statement 127
priority, operator 101
program
    executable 4, 12
    object 4
    source 3
program maintenance 17, 147
programming
    disciplined 9, 12
    top-down 18
progression
    arithmetic 20
    geometric 20

protected mode 203
publics 169
PUT BASIC statement 135
putc( ) function 28
putch( ) function 49, 127
put( ) example function 136
puthex( ) example function 67
puts( ) function 127
queue 112
radix 193
rand( ) function 105
random seed example 111
record, null 137
redirection 124, 128
reference, unresolved 174
register, segment 69, 202
registers
    CS 202
    DS 202
    ES 202
    SS 202
register storage class 73
relational expression 38
relational operator 15
response file 166
return statement 40, 46, 47, 48
reverse string example 111
ring up example program 50
S memory model 164, 165, 169, 202
scanf( ) function 38, 40, 51, 127, 177
scope 23, 68, 72
search example 117
segment
    code 164, 202
    data 164, 202
    extra 164, 202
    stack 164, 202
segment address 69, 159, 182, 196, 201
segment register 69, 202
short type 62, 126, 128
single-dimensioned array 78
single-precision type 34, 62
sizeof operator 98, 136, 148
sort, bubble 86
sort( ) example function 87
sorting 86
sort key 86
source program 3
space
    address 201
    white 128, 129
special print example program 140
specification, conversion 103, 124, 125, 171, 191
square root example 149
srand( ) function 106

209

SS register 202
stack 72, 176
stack segment 164, 202
standard, ANSI 9
standard input device 128
standard output device 124
statements 190
   assignment 15, 33, 81
   break 21, 116
   compound 11, 36, 38
   continue 21, 117
   else if 20, 109
   executable 46
   goto 16, 39
   if else 13, 35, 41, 54, 79, 93
   null 112
   return 40, 46, 47, 48
   switch 20, 113, 118, 119
statements, BASIC
   CLOSE 132
   DEF FN 23
   DIM 27, 77
   FIELD 134
   FOR 14, 37
   GET 137
   GOTO 16, 21, 39, 109
   IF-THEN-ELSE 13, 19, 20, 35, 103
   INPUT 28, 127, 135
   INPUT # 131
   LET 15
   LPRINT 139
   LSET 135
   NEXT 14, 37
   OPEN 130, 133
   OPTION BASE 27
   PRINT 28, 124, 127
   PRINT # 132
   PRINT USING 127
   PUT 135
   WEND 14, 38
   WHILE 14, 38
static storage class 56, 70, 71
stdio.h file 130, 146, 151
storage class 68, 189
   auto 72, 176
   extern 69, 70
   register 73
   static 56, 70, 71
strcat( ) function 142
strcpy( ) function 79
string 25, 48, 63, 78, 82
   control 124, 128
   mode 131, 134

string array, BASIC 63
string constant 13
strlen( ) function 99, 142
struct type 25, 64, 87
structure 10, 18, 19, 20, 24
   data 25, 64, 132, 134
studs( ) example function 46
sum( ) example function 51
switch statement 20, 113, 118, 119
symbolic constant 50, 87, 199
table, translation 56
tag 65, 87
taxcomp( ) example function 52
text editor, EDLIN 161
theory, hexadecimal number 193
three-dimensioned array 77
TI Business-Pro microcomputer 202
time( ) example function 81
top-down programming 18
translated mode 131
translation table 56
transportability 9, 123
two-dimensioned array 78
type 12, 26, 33, 47, 189
   char 48, 63, 126
   double 34, 62, 126
   double-precision 62
   float 33, 62, 126
   int 61, 98, 126
   long float 62
   long int 61, 126, 137
   short 62, 126, 128
   single-precision 34, 62
   struct 25, 64, 87
   unsigned 62, 98, 126
type conversion, automatic 39
union 26, 66
unresolved reference 174
unsigned type 62, 98, 126
variable 12, 23, 33, 68
   integer 61
virtual memory 203
WEND BASIC statement 14, 38
WHILE BASIC statement 14, 38
while loop 14, 17, 38, 41, 105
white space 128, 129
word 73
write file 131
XOR BASIC operator 127

COMPUTE! Books

Ask your retailer for these **COMPUTE! Books** or order directly from **COMPUTE!**.

Call toll free (in US) **800-346-6767** (in NY 212-887-8525) or write COMPUTE! Books, P.O. Box 5038, F.D.R. Station, New York, NY 10150

Quantity	Title	Price*	Total
_____	Machine Language for Beginners (11-6)	$14.95	_____
_____	The Second Book of Machine Language (53-1)	$14.95	_____
_____	COMPUTE!'s Guide to Adventure Games (67-1)	$12.95	_____
_____	Computing Together: A Parents & Teachers Guide to Computing with Young Children (51-5)	$12.95	_____
_____	COMPUTE!'s Personal Telecomputing (47-7)	$12.95	_____
_____	BASIC Programs for Small Computers (38-8)	$12.95	_____
_____	Programmer's Reference Guide to the Color Computer (19-1)	$12.95	_____
_____	Home Energy Applications (10-8)	$14.95	_____
	The Home Computer Wars: An Insider's Account of Commodore and Jack Tramiel		
_____	Hardback (75-2)	$16.95	_____
_____	Paperback (78-7)	$ 9.95	_____
_____	The Book of BASIC (61-2)	$12.95	_____
_____	The Greatest Games: The 93 Best Computer Games of all Time (95-7)	$ 9.95	_____
_____	Investment Management with Your Personal Computer (005)	$14.95	_____
_____	40 Great Flight Simulator Adventures (022)	$ 9.95	_____
_____	100 Programs for Business and Professional Use (017-3)	$24.95	_____
_____	From BASIC to C (026)	$16.95	_____
_____	The Turbo Pascal Handbook (037)	$14.95	_____

* Add $2.00 per book for shipping and handling.
Outside US add $5.00 air mail or $2.00 surface mail.

NC residents add 4.5% sales tax. _____
Shipping & handling: $2.00/book _____
Total payment _____

All orders must be prepaid (check, charge, or money order).
All payments must be in US funds.
☐ Payment enclosed.
Charge   ☐ Visa   ☐ MasterCard   ☐ American Express

Acct. No. _____ Exp. Date _____
                                                                         (Required)
Name _____

Address _____

City _____ State _____ Zip _____

*Allow 4–5 weeks for delivery.
Prices and availability subject to change.
Current catalog available upon request.

If you've enjoyed the articles in this book, you'll find the same style and quality in every monthly issue of **COMPUTE!** Magazine. Use this form to order your subscription to **COMPUTE!**.

For Fastest Service
Call Our **Toll-Free** US Order Line
1-800-247-5470
In IA call 1-800-532-1272

COMPUTE!
P.O. Box 5038
F.D.R. Station
New York, NY 10150

My computer is:
☐ Commodore 64 or 128 ☐ TI-99/4A ☐ IBM PC or PCjr ☐ VIC-20
☐ Apple ☐ Atari ☐ Amiga ☐ Other _____
☐ Don't yet have one...

☐ $24 One Year US Subscription
☐ $45 Two Year US Subscription
☐ $65 Three Year US Subscription

Subscription rates outside the US:
☐ $30 Canada and Foreign Surface Mail
☐ $65 Foreign Air Delivery

Name _____
Address _____
City _____ State _____ Zip _____
Country _____

Payment must be in US funds drawn on a US bank, international money order, or charge card.
☐ Payment Enclosed   ☐ Visa
☐ MasterCard   ☐ American Express

Acct. No. _____ Expires ____/____
                                    (Required)

Your subscription will begin with the next available issue. Please allow 4–6 weeks for delivery of first issue. Subscription prices subject to change at any time.

43122033